Entrepreneurship in Training

**CRITICAL ISSUES FACING
THE MULTINATIONAL ENTERPRISE**

Brian Toyne, Series Editor

Multinationals and
Canada—United States Free Trade
by Alan M. Rugman

International Business
and Governments:
Issues and Institutions
by Jack N. Behrman and Robert E. Grosse

Entrepreneurship in Training:
The Multinational Corporation in Mexico and Canada
by Michael A. DiConti

Entrepreneurship in Training

The Multinational Corporation in Mexico and Canada

by

Michael A. DiConti

University of South Carolina Press

to Norm

Library of Congress Cataloging-in-Publication Data

DiConti, Michael A., 1958–
    Entrepreneurship in training : the multinational corporation in
Mexico and Canada / by Michael A. DiConti.
        p.   cm. — (Critical issues facing the multinational
enterprise)
    Includes bibliographical references and index.
    ISBN 0-87249-818-2 (alk. paper)
    1. International business enterprises—Mexico—Case studies.
2. Entrepreneurship—Mexico—Case studies. 3. International
business enterprises—Canada—Case studies. 4. Entrepreneurship—
Canada—Case studies. 5. Control Data Corporation. I. Title.
II. Series.
HD2755.5.D53   1992
338'.04'0971—dc20   91-42535

Contents

Tables

Series Editor's Preface

The purpose of this series is to explore the multifaceted relationship of multinational enterprises (MNEs) with their global environment. Essentially, each book in the series is written by an expert and addresses a single issue of recognizable concern to MNEs. Thus, the aim of each book is to draw together and present the views of the various groups interested in the issue in a way that presents constructive suggestions for multinationals, irrespective of their nationality and inherent interests. Toward this end, each issue will be placed in its historical setting and explored from the perspective of the MNEs, their home countries, and the host countries in which they operate—where they agree and where they disagree, and why. Of particular concern will be the differences that have emerged or are emerging, by region (even by country when necessary), and among multinationals from different parts of the world.

Thoughtful practitioners will find the series helpful in developing a better understanding of the organizations they work for and interact or compete with. They will also gain a much better appreciation of the extent of the MNE's social, economic, and political influence. Specifically, the series is designed to provide a "library" of the many views taken toward the multinational by the governments, labor organizations, and the societies in which they operate or intend to operate and the reasons for these differing views.

Educators will also find the series of value as a supplemental set of readers for such topics in business administration, economics, international relations, and political science courses. Because of the scope of the series and its historical perspective, students will eventually have access to an extensive and thorough analysis of the MNE, the role it plays, the influence it has on the global economic and political order and thus the way it is viewed by other societal organizations.

The topic of *Entrepreneurship in Training: The Multinational Corporation in Mexico and Canada* by Michael A. DiConti is both timely and important since it sheds light on the key assertions made by supporters of dependency theory and modernization theory.

Briefly put, dependency theory argues that MNEs impede the economic development of countries in which they operate by stifling indigenous entrepreneurship. In stark contrast, modernization theory argues that MNEs stimulate local entrepreneurship. This book investigates these counterpoised arguments and concludes that MNEs not only spur local economic growth but also contribute to the distinctly national and populist goal of greater economic self-sufficiency. Consequently, it is definitely "required reading" by those directly or indirectly involved in the ongoing debate on the contributions made by MNEs to the development of local entrepreneurship. It should be of considerable interest to political scientists, economists, public policy-makers, and business decision-makers.

Brian Toyne
Series Editor

Preface

The influence of the multinational corporation (MNC) upon indigenous entrepreneurship in dependent countries is investigated in order to assess the validity of key assertions of dependency theory and modernization theory, the predominant and counterpoised theories of underdevelopment in the field of international political economy.

Dependency theorists cite the MNC subsidiary as the primary instrument by which development is impeded, claiming that multinational investment stifles indigenous entrepreneurship through a monopolistic control of host country markets. They seek to exclude the MNC from the economies of underdeveloped countries as a critical step in pursuing an autonomous and socialist path to development.

Alternatively, modernization theorists contend that stagnation is internally generated by entrenched elites, oppressive bureaucracies, and inefficient political and economic institutions, which support the status quo and inhibit indigenous capital formation. Modernization theorists favor multinational investment, viewing it as an effective vehicle for providing the technology, capital, and credible model to motivate greater indigenous entrepreneurship and departure from traditional and inefficient business practices.

The MNC's effects upon indigenous entrepreneurship are evaluated through a systematic examination of the Mexican and Canadian subsidiaries of Control Data Corporation (CDC), a large multinational computer company headquartered in the United States, representing a selection of nations and industry with high levels of dependence upon U.S. capital and trade.

Interviews with Canadian and Mexican entrepreneurs and CDC subsidiary executives yield results consistently supporting modernization theory, demonstrating means by which the MNC subsidiary may stimulate indigenous industrial entrepreneurship, and, thereby, the goal of increased national autonomy and development. The most prominent effect is demonstrated through CDC's employment of significant numbers of indigenous managers who later depart to initiate their own successful business ventures. Specifically, the managerial experience, technological background, and international exposure obtained through CDC employment are found to be important determining factors of future entrepreneurial success for indigenous managers. Furthermore, contrary to expectations consistent with dependency theory, little evidence that CDC's subsidiary operations serve to inhibit or displace indigenous entrepreneurship is discovered.

It is concluded that national policies which restrict multinational investment should be relaxed and supplemented by free-market-oriented institutional reforms to support the important development mission of fostering indigenous entrepreneurship in dependent states.

Acknowledgments

This work is a revision of my dissertation, completed in 1990 while I was a graduate student in political science at The Johns Hopkins University in Baltimore, Maryland. Any favorable criticism the work might attract is attributable in large measure to my advisers, Professor Charles F. Doran of Johns Hopkins and Professor Michael W. Doyle of Princeton University. Their insights and suggestions were critical in focusing my research and guiding my writing.

Professor Doran was particularly instrumental in the development of this work, especially for stimulating my interest in the subject area through a lecture given on dependency theory in his political economy seminar. Professor Doran also helped by introducing me to Mr. David Stothers, his former student and a current employee of Control Data Corporation. Mr. Stothers expended considerable effort on my behalf, and, most significantly, established contacts with the Mexican and Canadian subsidiaries of Control Data. His help is greatly appreciated.

I also extend special thanks to the Mexican and Canadian entrepreneurs I had the pleasure of interviewing during the course of the research. The opportunity to learn firsthand of their remarkable professional experiences enhanced my already considerable admiration for the entrepreneurial spirit.

Professor Doyle left Hopkins for Princeton midway through my graduate term, but, fortunately, Princeton's gain was not my loss. Professor Doyle continued to provide prompt and incisive feedback on my research, and later offered greatly appreciated encouragement and advice as I sought to publish my findings.

I am also grateful to the Institute for the Study of World Politics in Washington, D.C., whose generous fellowship paid for my travel to Mexico and Canada and also contributed to my support during the writing of the dissertation.

Entrepreneurship
in Training

Introduction

Growth and development are enduring features of the international economic landscape. However, global development has been uneven, and progress does not characterize the experience of many less developed countries (LDCs). Tragically, widespread malnutrition and recurrent famine plague the least advantaged LDCs, while among the less destitute, few can realistically hope to escape from poverty in the foreseeable future.

Protracted hardship among the LDCs has generated great popular disenchantment—amplified through inevitable comparison with the better fortune of advanced, industrialized countries. As a consequence, frustrated ambitions frequently give rise to violent struggles that sweep across national borders, accounting for the prominence that scholars of international relations accord to development issues.

Various causes of lagging development have been identified. Historically, capitalist imperialism and societal traditionalism were foremost, respectively representing forces originating externally and internally to the underdeveloped state.

In the recent, postcolonial decades, many of those who attribute continued responsibility to external sources (dependency theorists) cite the subsidiary of the multinational corporation as the primary instrument by which development is impeded, claiming that multinational business stifles indigenous initiative through its domination of host country markets, repatriating the resultant profits abroad.

Taking issue with this perspective, modernization theorists contend that prolonged stagnation is internally generated. Modernization theory favors multinational investment, viewing it as a powerful vehicle for providing underdeveloped countries with the technology, capital, and credible model to create greater indigenous initiative and depart from traditional and inefficient business practices.

Given their recognition that stagnant economies are characterized by depressed indigenous initiative, dependency and modernization theories are poised to be evaluated against this common dimension through a systematic investigation of the effects of the multinational

1

corporation (MNC)—with an aim to test competing claims of the two perspectives on underdevelopment. Specifically, the book examines the MNC subsidiary's effect upon indigenous initiative, formally embodied in business entrepreneurship—a recognized vanguard of self-directed and sustained national development.

Chapter 1 surveys the historical progression of development theory, giving greatest attention to the literature emerging since World War II. During this period, the LDCs' previously neglected and distinctive development problems have been extensively studied, in part reflecting the Third World's upgraded strategic value to the political and economic welfare of advanced, industrialized countries.

Next, dependency theory and modernization theory are recognized as the dominant contending perspectives on underdevelopment in the field of international political economy today. Although in dispute regarding the causes of and cures for underdevelopment and stagnation, dependency and modernization theories are shown to concur that sustained development must be characterized by the growth of indigenous entrepreneurship and lessened external dependence.

Chapter 2 demonstrates the prominence of entrepreneurship as the key causal agent of development in the scholarly literature of the field. Modernization and dependency theories are shown to give entrepreneurship central focus, although the competing doctrines strongly dispute the appropriate means for nurturing its growth.

In Chapter 3, the MNC subsidiary is highlighted as the focal point of the contending perspectives in their programs to promote indigenous entrepreneurship. In order to evaluate their competing development strategies, the recent record of state policies designed to promote indigenous entrepreneurship is analyzed. Not surprisingly, dependency and modernization theorists differ in their judgment of this record; however, the recent trend among developing countries of reducing restrictions on multinational investment demonstrates growing dissatisfaction with autarkic policies, motivating new consideration of the MNC's impact.

Formally, this book evaluates the key hypotheses generated by the contending perspectives with respect to the MNC subsidiary's effects upon indigenous entrepreneurship, employing a systematic methodology and utilizing empirical testing where feasible.[1] Substantively, these effects are broadly classified as exerting their influence either upon potential entrepreneurs or upon preexisting entrepreneurs.

In Chapter 4, the key hypotheses are operationally defined.

They are then applied to the examination of the activities of the Mexican and Canadian subsidiaries of Control Data Corporation (CDC), a large multinational computer company headquartered in the United States. Mexico and Canada were chosen for study because they represent nations with high levels of dependence upon the U.S. economy. In both countries, this dependence is manifest in a high concentration of trading activity with the United States and a high level of U.S. ownership in domestic industry. The Mexican and Canadian computer industries are representative of this relationship—controlled predominantly by U.S. capital. Thus, multinational investment is scrutinized under conditions of pronounced external dependence, giving force to possible results that may indicate its positive role in stimulating entrepreneurial activity.

The results of the investigation of CDC's subsidiaries are presented in Chapter 5, derived primarily from data obtained through interviews with CDC executives and indigenous entrepreneurs in Mexico and Canada. Subsidiary executives were extensively queried regarding the possible direct or indirect role of CDC in stimulating or depressing indigenous business enterprise. All of the interviewed entrepreneurs are former CDC employees. The professional experiences and achievements of each are thoroughly analyzed to assay the potential benefit or detriment of CDC to their subsequent commercial success.

The results are utilized to assess the relative validity of the modernization and dependency perspectives with respect to the impact of multinational investment upon indigenous entrepreneurship.

In Chapter 6, the findings are employed as a basis for evaluating the ability of Mexican and Canadian state policies to achieve the goal of increased indigenous entrepreneurial activity. Where policies are judged to be deficient, alternative directions are proposed.

The results of this investigation of CDC's Mexican and Canadian subsidiaries offer consistent support for modernization theory. CDC's most prominent effect upon indigenous entrepreneurship is manifested through its employment of significant numbers of indigenous managers who later depart to initiate their own successful business ventures in Mexico and Canada. The managerial experience, technological background, and international exposure obtained through CDC employment are discovered to be important determining factors of this future entrepreneurial success.

Additional confirmation of modernization theory is derived from the lack of evidence supporting dependency theory. No evidence that CDC's Mexican or Canadian operations serve to preempt potential entrepreneurship or displace preexisting entrepreneurship is discovered.

Based upon these findings, Mexican and Canadian policies that either prohibit or constrain multinational investment are claimed to retard indigenous entrepreneurship in dependent states. Particularly harmful are the limitations imposed on multinational investment in those industries where requisite indigenous skills or production capacities are deficient, as in the Mexican and Canadian computer industries. Thus, more liberal treatment of foreign direct investment is counseled, so as to allow multinational business to flourish.

It is also concluded that development will proceed most rapidly if policies to promote easier taxes, less bureaucratic red tape, and stable property rights are implemented, motivating greater private initiative. Additional reforms should include the privatization of highly subsidized and inefficient public enterprises, serving to redirect scarce resources to meet the increased capital requirements of an expanding and thriving indigenous entrepreneurial sector. The favorable consequence will be greater national self-reliance, advancing the prospects for strong, enduring, and less dependent development.

CHAPTER 1

Stagnation and Development

The study of development is motivated by the prevalence of poverty and stagnant growth among less developed countries, warranting an initial survey of the starting point from which future progress must proceed.

Underdevelopment—The Scope

Of some five billion world inhabitants, approximately 1.2 billion live in the so-called "developed" world comprising North America, Europe, the Soviet Union, Japan, Australia, South Africa, and New Zealand.[1] Regrettably, the characteristic wealth of developed societies is not experienced by the wide majority of the remaining 3.8 billion world inhabitants—residents of the "less developed countries" (LDCs).[2] While among themselves, the LDCs span a broad range of income levels,[3] more than half of the world's LDC population lives in countries with per capita incomes of less than $270.[4] The full extent of poverty is even more pronounced, attested to by the wide income disparities found within most LDCs. For instance, Montek Ahluwalia has observed that "while the poorest 40 percent of the population receives 25 percent of national income in developed Communist countries and 16 percent of the income in the developed capitalist countries, they receive only 12.5 percent of the much smaller income in the developing, capitalist countries and, in half of these countries, only 9 percent."[5]

Taken in tandem, LDC inequality and typically low national incomes account for the often cited World Bank estimate that 40 percent of the population in the Third World is in absolute poverty.[6] William Murdoch, in *The Poverty of Nations,* reports that half of the Third World's population is malnourished, life expectancy is less than 50 years, and more than 15 out of every hundred children born die before they are a year old.[7]

Few would claim that strong prospects exist for the swift amelioration of poverty. Yet over the long horizon, it is conceivable that a protracted trend of reduced population growth coupled with steady income gains will eliminate most of it. Of course, the possibility for such progress is indeterminate; yet, despite a host of gloomy forecasts predicting future expansion of LDC poverty,[8] Ian Little has reported on less scrutinized social indicators which support the view that the poor are now better off than at any time before, allowing a more sanguine vision of the future: "Life expectancy has risen everywhere from 1960 to 1978, from forty-two to fifty years in the World Bank's low income LDCs, and from fifty-four to sixty-one years in the middle income LDCs. In the same two groups, primary school enrollment has risen from 54 to 77 percent and from 81 to 97 percent respectively."[9]

Similarly, the composite Physical Quality of Life Index (PQLI), designed to measure physical well-being, increased for every Latin American country between 1960 and 1980.[10] Worldwide over the same 20-year period, it also has been found that low income, middle income, and industrial market country groups all experienced marked improvement in PQLI scores, with the most dramatic increase occurring in the low income group.[11] Taken together, these recent improvements provide hope for future advances in the condition of the poor. Nonetheless, per capita income, longevity, health, and literacy indicators are capable of measuring only the physical dimensions of well-being.

Subjective measures are also relevant welfare indicators. For instance, cross-country data measuring happiness demonstrate no tendency for inhabitants of wealthy countries to be happier on average than inhabitants of poor countries; however, within a country, happiness is found to be correlated with income position.[12] These findings imply that the desire to maximize one's absolute welfare is mediated by a competing desire to maximize relative welfare. In discussing relative standing, measures of income inequality are relevant. For instance, among 96 LDCs between 1958 and 1978, population-weighted Gini coefficients increased from 0.41 to 0.54,[13] demonstrating increasing inequality within these countries over time. These data are discouraging; they moderate Little's otherwise hopeful findings that "for the past twenty-five to thirty years [up to 1982], growth of per caput incomes has been much higher for most LDCs than in any other historical period"[14] and that "per caput real products in LDCs rose at an annual rate of 3.1 percent from 1970 to 1979, as against 2.5 percent per annum for the more developed countries."[15]

Therefore, in the context of rising intrastate inequality, the unfortunate consequence is that much of the benefit of LDC per capita income growth eluded the poor.[16] In the worst cases, economic position stagnated in absolute terms and deteriorated relatively.

International Political Economy and Development

For the political scientist engaged in the examination of development and stagnation, both absolute and relative standards of well-being are scrutinized. The economist, in contrast, traditionally defers on the dynamics of distribution, limiting his/her purview to goals of societal wealth maximization.[17] Political science, concerned as it is with the dynamics of inter-and intra-societal power configurations, necessarily includes the distributional question within its domain. Its quest in the study of development is to advance prescriptive models that strike a balance between absolute and relative dimensions of welfare, economic and otherwise. This is a difficult task, for although the goals are to illuminate means for maximizing overall wealth while diminishing inequality, the pursuit of one often inhibits the realization of the other. In such instances, stagnation and development may appear to coexist. For example, an increase in marginal tax rates targeting the wealthy may give rise to redistribution and the development goal of greater income equality, but the parallel, adverse effect may be a long-term stagnation in per capita incomes due to diminished investment incentives.[18] And the converse situation may also obtain, when per capita income growth is accompanied by increased income inequality—a frequent outcome among LDCs.

A political study of development also recognizes the superimposition of the international state system upon domestic welfare goals and policies. As Robert Gilpin argues in *U.S. Power and the Multinational Corporation,* the international context is political by nature and, therefore, relative.

> In a world in which power rests on wealth, changes in the relative distribution of wealth imply changes in the distribution of power and in the political system itself. This, in fact, is what is meant by saying politics is about relative gains. Politics concerns the efforts of groups to redistribute gains to their own advantage. ... Though all may be gaining or declining in absolute capability, what will concern states principally are the effects of their absolute gains on relative position.[19]

Thus, it is acknowledged that the domestic welfare goals of growth and equality must be harmonized with or subordinated to the greater imperatives determined by state competition within the international power hierarchy.

It becomes evident, then, that a robust study of development will involve careful consideration of the complex and interacting effects of both political and economic variables. Therefore, the field of international political economy is particularly suited to explore the broad issues of development, recognizing as it does the dynamic and reciprocal interactions of the political (relative) and economic (absolute) dimensions of the process.

Next, within the scope of international political economy, theories of development are highlighted and evaluated for their successes and failures in illuminating the path to progress for less developed countries.

Development Theory—History

A historical account of the intellectual progression of development theory appropriately commences with a discussion of the ideas of Adam Smith, David Ricardo, and Thomas R. Malthus—the prominent classical economists of the late 18th and early 19th centuries who watched England act as a wellspring for the Industrial Revolution. The phenomenon of industrial expansion and the great wealth generated drew the classical writers toward the goal of discovering its nature and causes. In their writings, the catalyzing agents of capital formation, savings rates, technological development, and market demand all figured prominently. Regarding political factors, however, the classical economists counseled government to adopt a limited, noninterventionist ("laissez-faire") position toward domestic private enterprise.[20] It is not unlikely that this minimalist position regarding government activism was conditioned in part by optimism generated from the great industrial success in advanced areas and also by the absence of clear failures of the new model in other parts of the world. According to Smith: "Little else is requisite to carry a state to the highest degree of opulence from the lowest barbarism, but peace, easy taxes, and a tolerable administration of justice, all the rest being equal."[21]

Despite such confidence, Smith, Ricardo, and Malthus each predicted the inevitable decay of capitalism[22] and, in describing the scenario of decline, acknowledged the great misery of the poorer masses. Smith adjures: "No society can surely be flourishing and happy, of which the far greater number of the members are poor and miserable. It is but equity, besides, that they who feed, cloath, and lodge the whole body of the people, should have such a share of the produce of their own labor as to be tolerably well fed and cloathed."[23]

Ricardo evinced similar concerns. In the context of his labor theory of value, he described the inequity and inherent rift between labor and capitalist in terms that Karl Marx would later seize upon: "The opinion entertained by the labouring class, that the employment of machinery is frequently detrimental to their interests, is not founded on prejudice and error, but is conformable to the correct principles of political economy."[24]

Though the classical economists noted that capitalism often failed the poor, each considered capitalism's "invisible hand" to be the best available mechanism for guiding societal progress and individual welfare. As a result, their primary scholarly activity was the task of discovering and detailing the means toward successful pursuit of per capita income growth, leaving the job of distribution to market benevolence.

Less pessimistic about the prospects for capitalism's demise were the marginalist and later the neoclassical economists,[25] who were able to observe and theoretically account for the dramatic and accelerating technological advancements characterizing the course of 19th-century industry—a development unforseen by the classical writers.

Neoclassical scholars departed from the classical economists' willingness to confront non-economic issues, restricting their scope to the more rigorous, albeit limited, methodology of deductive formalism based upon first principles (e.g., the Law of Supply and Demand, the Quantity Theory of Money).[26] Consequently, many of the problems of national development were too "messy" to address. In any case, characteristic neoclassical optimism took for granted an upward trend in development. Strong and lasting growth in the LDCs was expected to generate sufficient surplus to enrich capitalists and to remunerate labor adequately. Ideally, the economic role of government would be restricted to "natural" monopolies providing public goods and services. In the international realm, free trade and production according to comparative advantage would be the rule. A natural geographic extension of free trade would then bring the developing world within the prosperous domain of capitalist development.

Karl Marx shared the belief of the early classical writers regarding capitalism's demise, and in fact saw the end as quite imminent.

Also in common with the classical writers, Marx perceived a potentiality in capitalism for spurring modernization and economic growth in developing countries. Nonetheless, Marx saw capitalist development as exploitative by nature. Through its competitive character and immiseration of the proletarian masses, capitalism was laying the foundation for a popular socialist revolution. Thus, Marx's capitalism was progressive, but hopes for social and economic equality were to be deferred until the economic foundations of capitalism were toppled, for Marx saw social structures as being economically determined. Hence, social reform would necessarily await economic restructuring along non-capitalist lines.

Marx, the classical economists, and the early neoclassical economists were influenced by the economic and social institutions of England, Western Europe, and the United States. To these writers, the institutions only awaited transferral to the less developed world. Other than a matter of timing then, early development and later development were seen as proceeding along similar lines. While not all saw capitalism as benign in its social disruption (e.g., Marx, Malthus, and Ricardo), its expansion was considered inevitable, progressive, and, therefore, desirable for all countries—developed and developing alike.

Historical hindsight counters the classical and Marxist predictions of capitalism's morbid course. At the same time, however, the buoyant optimism of early neoclassical writers is equally difficult to vindicate considering the extent of contemporary Third World stagnation. The rapid expansion and prosperity characterizing early capitalist development have not taken hold among many of the LDCs on a scale necessary to eliminate the widespread and, in some cases, still expanding poverty found there.

Contemporary Development Theory

Against this background, contemporary development theory arose with its focus rooted upon Third World stagnation. Attention was long in coming; indeed, not really until after World War II was primary political weight accorded to Third World issues. Notwithstanding altruistic proclamations, the motives were essentially political. Colonial independence in the wake of bipolar competition launched a race for political and economic hegemony in the Third World between the United States and the Soviet Union. Foreign aid, direct investment, and military bases were among the tools adopted by the United States to deter Soviet military expansionism and the lure of communism in the Third World.

It soon came to be acknowledged that for many LDCs the problems associated with stagnant development were less tractable than previously assumed. In search of novel solutions, Third World scholarship turned from economically rooted models of growth to more politically oriented theories that aimed to outline the particular institutions, interests, and attitudes that affect LDC progress. Equally important, distributional issues achieved prominence—an intellectual acknowledgment of the political and social significance embedded in the observation that equality often suffers at the expense of growth.[27]

The "modernization" and "dependency" (or "dependencia," acknowledging the theory's Latin American roots) perspectives are the two schools of thought reigning dominant in contemporary scholarship on the political economy of development. Both perspectives cover a considerable range in their conclusions and prescriptions and stand in sharp contrast on many critical issues, providing stimulating dialogue in their analyses of Third World underdevelopment.

Modernization Theory

To the modernization theorist, economic development must be preceded by the transformation of a nation's traditional institutions, values, and cultural patterns into modern forms. Not only do traditional elements characterize LDCs, they also represent the primary impediments to development. In the absence of these impediments, development would unfold naturally. For instance, J. Samuel Valenzuela and Arturo Valenzuela argue of Latin America that "traditional attitudes and institutions stemming from the colonial past have proven to be serious, if not fatal, stumbling blocks to any indigenous effort to develop economically, socially, or politically. The values of aristocratic rural elites have contributed to 'irrational' patterns highly detrimental to modernization."[28]

Also with respect to Latin America, Seymour Lipset has concluded, citing a host of research studies, that "the comparative evidence from various nations of the Americas sustains the generalization that cultural values are among the major factors which affect the potentiality for economic development."[29] Of course, modernization theory is claimed to hold beyond Latin America, also to encompass Asia, Africa, and, indeed, all nations "plagued" by traditional structures.

Although modernization theory emerged in the 1950s to become the dominant form of development analysis, its intellectual substructure—the traditional/modern dichotomy—was based in 19th-century social thought.[30] In the early modernization writings, Western Europe provided the modern forms by which traditional societies were distinguished.

As a result of the inclusion of non-economic factors in its analysis, the emergence of modernization theory after World War II represented a noteworthy advance over neoclassical economics in addressing the problems of LDC stagnation. Seizing the modernization framework, social scientists from a variety of disciplines applied their methodologies to the study of stagnation and development.[31] As a result, the long recognized and lingering "economic" deficiencies of technological backwardness, low savings, low capital formation, and lack of entrepreneurship were each explained in social terms. To date, the approach has attracted considerable attention and many supporters. Lipset is prominent among post-World War II modernization theorists; he ascribes the economic deficiencies of LDCs to the barriers presented by traditional societal values and cultural traits. For example, in explaining the dearth of LDC entrepreneurship, Lipset describes the "lack of instrumental behavior, weak achievement orientation, and the disdain for the pragmatic and the material" as having "prevented the rise of a risk taking business sector oriented to rational competitive and bureaucratic enterprise."[32]

Recent historical evidence, however, convincingly counters the general applicability of Lipset's claims. For example, South Korea, a society that had been expected to be highly resistant to a course of sustained capitalist development, has defied skeptics and achieved unprecedented rates of growth while maintaining a culture and values that are highly traditional by Western standards. Japan's experience similarly counters the thesis that development requires the destruction of traditional values. George Masannat describes how, in fact, traditional values and customs were actually harnessed by the Japanese government to help facilitate development:

> Commitment to the Emperor, obedience to the family, the use and exploitation of the peasantry in the countryside in order to build and rapidly develop the urban industrial, economic and military sectors of the society, and the collectivistic orientation have been factors of great positive value to the modernization process. . . . Land reforms were not undertaken; the existing social, economic, and political elites in the

countryside were allowed, as far as it was possible, to enjoy their status and exercise their authority. The community and family system were reinforced and given new legal status and sanctions.[33]

More persuasive with respect to the significance of the traditional/modern dichotomy is the aspect of modernization theory that holds institutional traditionalism as responsible for inhibiting LDC progress. Typifying this perspective, R. Scott attributes underdevelopment in Latin America to political traditionalism, noting the "inability of Latin America's political structures to act as efficient integrating mechanisms."[34]

The institutionalist perspective has been forcefully and cogently articulated by Douglass C. North, an economic historian, who asserts that the political establishment of efficient "institutional arrangements and property rights" in Western Europe accounts for the rise of the Western World.[35] North refines rather than discards neoclassical economic theory, criticizing it as being limited in its ability to explain economic development due to its static nature and to its unrealistic simplifying assumptions of zero transaction costs and perfect and costless information. The critical result is a failure to recognize the value of making economic decisions via the political process.

> [Neoclassical theory] provides quite limited answers since it is immediately relevant to a world of perfect markets—that is, perfect in the sense of zero transaction costs: the costs of specifying the enforcing property rights. Yet we have come to realize that devising and enforcing a set of rules of the game is hardly ever costless and the nature of these costs is at the very root of all economic system's problems.[36]

North argues that efficient political organization and resulting institutional arrangements are necessary to provide positive inducements for individuals to engage in activities that lead to economic growth. In this respect, the activity of a responsive government in recognizing and enforcing tangible and intellectual property rights is designated by North as vital to and typical of those countries that have successfully pursued development. Without a full system of property rights, the expected profits from introducing new products or techniques are diminished, eroding commercial incentive and entrepreneurial initiative.

In the 18th century, first the Netherlands and then England developed the incentive structures necessary for sustained economic growth. In comparison, France and Spain failed to establish an efficient set of property rights, stifling innovation and the possibility for sustained growth.[37] In the Netherlands and England, the enforcement of property rights through land enclosures, patents, copyrights, and easier taxes provided incentives for entrepreneurs to develop new techniques and apply them in commercial enterprise. Thus, North concludes that "the industrial revolution was not the source of modern economic growth. It was the outcome of raising the private rate of return on developing new techniques and applying them to the production process."[38] Therefore, the inability of much of the Third World to effect development is ascribed by the institutionalist perspective to a political failure to implement efficient economic arrangements. Obversely, the institutionalist perspective attributes successful development to the political ability and willingness of a society to implement arrangements and rules that motivate and complement commercial enterprise. For example, the governments of South Korea and Japan have succeeded in directing their societies' energies toward vigorous, export-led growth through a variety of institutional measures. In the case of Japan, North observes that although values and practices remained highly traditional, industrialization and development were preceded by the modernization of the political control structure through "the emergence of a central bureaucratic authority with a professionally trained, rationally structured and achievement-oriented bureaucracy above a fragmented feudal system."[39]

The importance of amenable institutions was recognized by early scholars such as Smith, Malthus, Marx, and John Stuart Mill; however, they gave little regard to the possibility of strong and prolonged resistance on the part of many underdeveloped countries to the adoption of efficient economic forms. Rather, they were largely of the opinion that prolonged exposure to the developed Western world, whether indirectly through trade or directly through colonial occupation, would eventually bring about development. Clearly, those expectations have not been realized.

Regardless of the form and degree of LDC exposure to the developed societies, the modernization perspective imputes primary responsibility for post-colonial stagnation to factors within the LDC itself. Although certain adverse, dependent ties of colonial origin may still be maintained, LDC economic sovereignty is generally assumed. Any ill effects from external coercion are considered to be ancillary.

On the positive side, the modern, developed states are viewed as being agents of development in diffusing the culture of modernity into the developing societies. As Gary Gereffi explains:

> Both material benefits (capital and technology) and cultural patterns (institutions and values) are diffused or spread from the developed to the underdeveloped countries and within each underdeveloped nation from the modern to the traditional sectors. The material inputs are to be transmitted mainly through foreign investment and aid; cultural patterns such as democratic attitudes and modern entrepreneurship should be diffused through education and the mass media. The anticipated result is the elimination of these internal obstacles that prevented the underdeveloped societies from following the path already set by the advanced nations.[40]

By this description, progress for the late developing nations is externally catalyzed; failures are attached to entrenched and resistant strains of traditionalism, for which the LDCs themselves are presumed responsible. In this regard, the appeal of modernization theory to the advanced capitalist states is apparent, because it offers justification for their efforts to extend their political and economic influence into the post-colonial periphery.[41]

Structuralism and Dependency Theory

Not surprisingly, writers from the Third World were dissatisfied with modernization theory. The enshrinement of a Western European development model seemed ethnocentric. Furthermore, while a certain degree of modernization was considered necessary for a country to emerge from stagnation, traditional values and attitudes were not viewed as necessarily incompatible with or counterproductive to development.[42] Additionally, the lack of institutional transformation into more economically and socially efficient forms was blamed on forces of external dominance in their contentment with and support of the traditional status quo.

Structuralism and, later, dependency theory represented efforts to criticize modernization theory's assumptions and conclusions while forwarding alternative diagnoses of Third World stagnation.

Arising in the 1950s, the structuralist argument held that the "liberal" capitalist world economy tended to preserve or even increase inequalities between developed and less developed countries.[43] Trade as the "engine of growth," characterizing the experience of developing countries of the 19th century, was no longer seen to be an available mechanism for the diffusion of development. Raul Prebisch, as director of the United Nations Economic Commission for Latin America (ECLA), prominently articulated the tenets of structuralism in the late 1950s;[44] however, not until 1964 did he gain an international audience for the structuralist position, with his appointment as secretary general of the United Nations Conference on Trade and Development (UNCTAD) and his presentation of a report entitled "Towards a New Trade Policy for Development." According to Robert Gilpin, the "heart" of the structuralist argument is that:

> the nature of technical advance, cyclical price movements, and differences in demands for industrial goods and primary products cause a secular deterioration in the terms of trade for commodity exporters, that is, deterioration of the prices the LDCs receive for their commodity exports relative to the prices of the manufactured goods they import from developed countries. . . . As a consequence of this secular decline, the peripheral economies are forced to export ever-larger quantities of food and commodities to finance the import of manufactured goods from industrial countries.[45]

Structuralists concluded that the primary benefits of international trade were largely eroded through the deterioration of the terms of trade for LDC exports.[46] The leading strategy for escape from the structural predicament was the promotion of "import-substitution industrialization" (I-S-I) among LDCs. By this strategy, the domestic production of previously imported manufactures was to be supported through import tariffs, industrial subsidies, and encouragement of foreign investment in manufacturing. These schemes were widely applied by LDCs beginning in the 1950s, but they met with little apparent success and were widely criticized as ineffective and even deleterious to development. Notably, I-S-I policies were typically unable to achieve their intention of decreasing import reliance. Domestic finished-goods manufacturers often required large imports of capital-intensive, intermediate inputs. This requirement generated increased foreign exchange needs, putting additional pressure on commodity producers to increase exports. Fledgling domestic producers were protected from imports and as a result felt little motivation to become price competitive internationally. Thus, most indigenous manufacturers were unable to export, and they languished in the high cost domestic market[47]—at considerable expense to the home consumer.

But perhaps most criticized of I-S-I policies was the attraction of great numbers of subsidiaries of multinational corporations (MNCs) into the Third World. These organizations were often concentrated by industry and highly visible, serving as easy scapegoats for failing economies. Lagging development was blamed on foreign corporate control, a perception which stimulated the call for the expropriation and future exclusion of foreign direct investment (fdi). Since the anticipated economic advance of the Third World was not precipitated by I-S-I strategies, a more nationalistic theory of stagnation and development—dependency theory—emerged in the mid-1960s.

Although dependency theory is often described as being a reaction to the policies advocated by the structuralists, the two approaches have much in common. Both are strongly postured against the tenets of modernization theory, denying the natural "diffusion" of development from the developed to the less developed countries. Similarly, both perspectives believe that LDCs have much to lose from their acquiescent integration into the liberal, capitalist international system. But dependency theory was more radical in its diagnosis of the problems associated with LDC stagnation. While an LDC's inferior position within the international capitalist economy was seen as limiting, dependency theorists argued that the structuralist solution of domestic reform (import substitution) could not controvert the fundamental economic and political inequities between advanced and Third World countries.

The fundamental thesis of dependency theory is that the dependence of LDCs upon advanced capitalist nations causes underdevelopment and stagnation. Osvaldo Sunkel, in "Big Business and Dependencia," cites numerous means of domination that are claimed to support and extend dependent relations: "tied loans, technical aid, preferential arrangements with regard to transportation, communication, foreign investment, tariffs and so on."[48] Unlike structuralists, dependency theorists perceive little flexibility for the individual LDC to advance its international position through capitalist means. Andre Gunder Frank asserts a strong dependency position in stating, "It is capitalism, both world and national, which produced underdevelopment in the past and which still generates underdevelopment in the present."[49] Various other dependency theorists do allow for the possibility of limited development within LDCs; nonetheless, the overriding outcome is continued dependence, for any such development is externally conditioned and, therefore, distorted and incomplete. Theotonio Dos Santos describes the dynamic:

> Dependence is a conditioning situation in which the economies of one group of countries are conditioned by the development and expansion of others. A relationship of interdependence between two or more economies or between such economies and the world trading system becomes a dependent relationship when some countries can expand through self-impulsion while others, being in a dependent position, can only expand as a reflection of the expansion of the dominant countries, which may have positive or negative effects on their immediate development.[50]

Despite similarities with Marxism, the limitations that dependency theory attributes to the capitalist mode of development are fundamental, marking an important contrast. In fact, contemporary Marxists might argue that "some Third World countries are developing and becoming industrialized,"[51] consistent with Marx's claim that eventually "the bourgeoisie, by the rapid improvements of production, by the immensely facilitated means of communication, draws all, even the most barbarian nations into civilization."[52] Marx viewed capitalism as historically progressive, with its international unfolding as essential, thereby laying the foundations for social revolution and world communism. In this respect, Geoffrey Kay suggests that a Marxist explanation for continued LDC stagnation might read that "capital created underdevelopment not because it exploited the underdeveloped world, but because it did not exploit it enough."[53]

Unlike Marxism, dependency theory denies the availability of progressive, "diffusionist" capitalist mechanisms for LDC development. Dependency theorists advocate various means to overcome dependency; however, the most commonly advocated solution is socialist revolution, which is seen as a means to effect a separation from the international capitalist system.[54] Less radical means that are advocated to promote Third World development include economic regionalism, the formation of commodity cartels, and the demand for a "New International Economic Order." Fundamental to all dependency approaches, whether socialist or capitalist, is an attempt to alter the LDCs' political and economic relationship with the developed world. Thus, the initial development goal is to gain a measure of autonomy—whether autonomy within the capitalist system or autonomy outside the capitalist system—through altering the traditional bonds of dependence to the advanced states. Once the development goal of greater autonomy is achieved, developmental goals of economic growth and equitable wealth distribution may be advanced.

Of the four dependency reduction strategies cited above, socialist revolution is the most radical. To socialist strategists, whether stagnation and underdevelopment[55] or "associated-dependent development"[56] best characterizes a particular LDC's development pattern, its subordinated role is seen as irreversibly perpetuated by its historically depressed economic standing. In short, dependency is "structurally" inescapable within the international capitalist system; therefore, only complete withdrawal will enable the achievement of independent, balanced, self-propelled, and sustained development. While it is not generally promised that socialism will provide an economy with greater absolute wealth than capitalist dependent development, dependency theories attach greater priority to political, non-economic measures of development. Thus, socialist revolution is seen as providing the greatest prospect for the erosion of domestic inequalities through wealth distribution and class obliteration. Furthermore, insularity from international capitalism confers the development goal of political and economic autonomy to the socialist state. Of course, autonomy in its own right is satisfying, but autonomous development also allows for a domestic definition of the particular development features to be pursued.

Dependency and Modernization Theories Evaluated

As alternatives to socialism, non-revolutionary dependency solutions represent attempts to refashion the pattern of dependent capitalist relationships. Each solution advocates inter-LDC alliances, forged to shift economic power from the developed states to themselves. Attempts to organize along these lines have achieved little success.

For instance, economic regionalism in the Third World has generated little benefit when compared to the European Economic Community. Third World or South-South trade did not grow significantly in the 1970s and in the early 1980s,[57] and for years to come the developed countries are expected to continue as the major importers of Third World products.

Likewise, the strategy of commodity cartelization has met with very limited success in the Third World, with the Organization of Petroleum Exporting Countries being the outstanding exception. Paul Eckbo has documented 51 attempts at cartelization of raw materials; only 19 succeeded in achieving "oligopoly rents" (exceptional profits derived from holding prices substantially above the marginal cost of production). Furthermore, the "successful" cartels only had an average life of 4 to 5 years.[58] In any case, Third World cartelization hardly promotes development among resource-poor LDCs. Significantly, the hardest hit from the oil crises of the 1970s were clearly the non-oil-producing LDCs.

The 1974 call for a New International Economic Order (NIEO) by the "Group of 77" developing nations at the Sixth Special Session of the United Nations General Assembly was a demand for the implementation of international policy reforms that would shift economic advantage to the LDCs. Reforms were to include LDC debt alleviation, greater foreign aid flows from developed states, lower cost and increased Western technology flows, and agreements to reverse declining terms of trade for raw material exports.[59] Across the board, the NIEO demands have not been met by the developed states, nor do they seem to hold any serious prospect of future realization.

Together, the record of economic regionalism, commodity cartelization, and the NIEO provides little hope that similar LDC alliances will be able to wrest significant economic power or substantial benefit from the advanced countries in the future. LDC infighting, competition, and goal diversity all mitigate against possibilities for unified and successful regionalization or cartelization. Furthermore, while NIEO calls for distributive justice may provoke a degree of guilt among wealthy states, requests for "due compensation" merit little hope for fulfillment.

Although framed by dependency theorists, LDC alliance solutions hearken back to ECLA structuralism in that they offer initiatives to rectify international wealth imbalances—within the capitalist setting. Also, LDC alliance solutions share structuralism's dismal performance record. Quite probably, these disappointments have served to reinforce and popularize dependency theory's more radical aim— to effect socialist revolution among LDCs as a necessary first step toward development.

Of course, the record of success resulting from socialist revolution is also poor. While economic inequalities within the communist countries have been described as less pronounced than in advanced, capitalist countries, communist median living standards pale in comparison and are largely responsible for the recent profound changes in the economic and political foundations of the former communist countries of Eastern Europe and the Soviet Union, marking the end of Soviet communism's reign as the preferred socialist model for revolutionary countries.

Dependency theorists view the collapsing communist regimes as representing failures in the chosen form and the implementation of socialist revolution rather than repudiations of their vision for a restructured society. Thus, while communist and former communist countries are today more vigorously pursuing economic links with capitalist countries and, domestically, are seeking to adopt, albeit still in limited quantity, private property, profit incentives, and competitive pricing, dependencistas still consider socialist revolution, if faithfully executed and sustained, to be the best means for escaping the exploitative and stultifying hegemony of international capitalism.

Whereas the radical solution to dependency is autonomy achieved through socialist revolution, the modernization perspective views interdependence as the solution to dependence. In this scheme, greater self-reliance is sought rather than complete autonomy or independence.

Interdependence, defined as mutual dependence, characterizes the contemporary international position of advanced capitalist states. While the modernization approach acknowledges the relative dependence of LDCs, it claims that the alternative of socialist revolution leads to depressed development. For maximum LDC development, modernization theorists assert that an initial position of dependence may be leveraged through domestic policies of economic liberalization and political receptiveness to benefits diffusing from the developed states. In the course of development, decreased asymmetries in dependence between nations evolve, with the more dependent in turn gaining in self-reliance, a capacity allowing for the self-directed pursuit of development goals. Thus, according to the modernization perspective, interdependence may provide what Chung-in Moon has called "leverage for the weak," with gains in LDC self-reliance providing for satisfaction of political aims comparable to those rendered by complete autonomy, while at the same time delivering the superior fruits of liberal capitalism.[60] Gereffi further elaborates this viewpoint:

Some believe, like A. O. Hirschman (1978), that the asymmetries
in economic relations among nations implied by dependency often contain the "seeds of their own destruction"—i.e., countervailing dialecti-
cal forces that would transform an asymmetrical relation not into its
Hegelian opposite but at least into a relation where the initial asymme-
try is considerably reduced or perhaps even eliminated.[61]

In this manner, LDCs are perceived as capable of pursuing a
dependent path to a robust and increasingly self-reliant pattern of
development. The process is gradual and incremental, as the tide of
capitalist progress transforms dependence into balanced interdependence.

Observations drawn from contemporary society disclose increasing levels of interdependence among states. For example, Robert
Keohane and Joseph Nye, in a 1987 article reevaluating their classic
work *Power and Interdependence,* claim that interdependence
among states has become more extensive in the past decade, reinforced by the diminishing role of military force. As evidence, they
cite more diffused world trade shares, increased national sensitivity
to finance and trade shocks, the easing of the Cold War, and arms
control progress.[62]

As power becomes less concentrated through evolving interdependence, LDCs are expected to obtain increased advantage from
economic liberalization, capturing a greater share of the benefits from
their trading partners. In addition, expanding international linkages
are expected to lead to even greater levels of domestic modernization, as national elites are subjected to external competition, weaken-
ing their control over traditional markets and institutions. Furthermore, Larry Diamond argues that increasingly "denser links with the
West fuel democracy," since other political forms come to be exposed
as either lacking "strong legitimizing principles" (autocracy) or as
being associated with unsuccessful economic outcomes (communism).[63]

On the contrary, dependencistas deny that expanded linkages
with the developed economies will bring about increased self-reliance
and an erosion of dependence among developing countries. They
doubt that balanced interdependence will be a consequence of the
economic liberalization and political programs that modernization
theorists assert will succeed in reaping the fruits of enhanced international contact. Instead, they fear for the sovereignty of developing
countries, believing that increased linkages will only bring further

dependence, thereby essentially replicating the historical process that gave rise to contemporary dependence. Thus, dependency theorists tend to deny the likelihood that dependent states will achieve self-impelled development within a framework of international capitalism.

Based upon the evidence, however, Jonathan Lemco has shown that the dependencistas' "pessimistic view is difficult to support."[64] South Korea and Taiwan have thrived as a result of industrialization programs which have relied upon external links forged in accord with export-oriented growth strategies. Dependency theorists, in contrast, tend to diminish the relevance of such "evidence" to the overall dependency paradigm. Most representative of this position is Fernando Henrique Cardoso, who has claimed that "empirical tests of dependency theory have largely missed the target because the tests have been ahistorical."[65] Unfortunately, historical empirical testing is exceedingly difficult and often impossible to undertake successfully, explaining why many dependency theorists have disavowed the empiricist/positivist tradition altogether, causing Cardoso to assert a failure to deliver in its "promise for a cumulative behavioral science."[66] This "post-positivist" orientation rejects the utility of empirical testing and scientific method in the social sciences. Instead, post-positivists support their beliefs regarding underdevelopment with insights derived from non-empirical historical analysis.[67]

The post-positivist orientation does allow for greater methodological pluralism in the search for truths, yet, as Thomas Biersteker claims, it suffers in providing an objective rationale for judging between alternative explanations:

> Post-positivist scholarship does not offer us any clear criteria for choosing among the multiple and competing explanations it produces. Once liberal toleration yields to the production of alternative interpretations and understandings, how are we to choose from the abundance of alternative explanations? How are we to judge whether interpretation A is to be preferred to interpretation B in a post-positivist era? How are we to ensure that post-positivist pluralism, in the absence of any alternative criteria, will avoid legitimizing ignorance, intolerance, or worse? ... As much as I welcome the openness and pluralism of post-positivism, I would like to see some explicit discussion of criteria for evaluating alternatives before I leap from the problematic terrain of positivism into what could turn out to be a post-positivist void.[68]

It is important to observe that dependency theorists are not monolithic in adherence to post-positivist anti-empiricism. Many dependency scholars do retain positivist methodology in their research and undertake research which is supportive of the dependency paradigm[69]—providing an essential common ground for the current work's evaluation of the contending theoretical perspectives.

Narrowing the Framework for Discourse

The modernization and dependency perspectives both claim to offer superior programs for provoking realization of the optimal balance among the three component development goals: autonomy, income equality, and economic growth.[70] In practice, the two perspectives offer differing "ideal" or "optimizing" mixes among the three goals, with modernization theory favoring economic growth and dependency theory favoring economic equality.[71] The third and probably most contentious development goal—autonomy—is variously conceived by development scholars. Dependency theorists assert that withdrawal from the world capitalist system increases the chance for political and economic autonomy; modernization writers perceive the typical socialist revolutionary process as merely a shift in alliances from dependent capitalism to dependent socialism (consider Cuba, a pre-revolutionary U.S. dependent and a post-revolutionary Soviet dependent). In addition, modernization theorists reject the goal of complete autonomy, emphasizing the benefits of linkage with the world capitalist economy. Through this linkage, they assert, greater self-reliance is achieved as the LDC develops, with its growing interdependence with developed countries providing the political and economic bases for maximized, self-directed development. This process is characterized as "dependency reversal." Dependency reversal, or reductions in dependency, flow "from the changes in power relations between strong and weak economic and political actors."[72] Robert Packenham argues that while not inevitable, dependency reversal within the capitalist world economy is seen by modernization theorists as far easier to achieve than the socialist transformation advocated by the dependency scholars.[73]

Many dependency writers have recently been more accepting of accumulating evidence that sustained economic growth, attended by reductions in income inequality, has been a feature of LDC capitalist development in certain countries (e.g., South Korea and Taiwan). In this acknowledgement, the "strong-form stagnationist" dependency contention (i.e., that economic growth, inequality, and autonomy are prevented by dependence) loses credibility. Martin Fransman aptly characterizes the intransigence of those continuing in the "rigid" viewpoint as engaging in what Imre Lakatos has referred to as a "degenerating scientific research program."[74]

Standing on more credible ground in the contemporary debate are those dependency theorists who do accept case evidence of LDC economic growth in combination with reduced income inequality, but who still insist, despite this acknowledgement, that dependence is not fundamentally altered. In fact, as Bill Warren has observed, their primary assertion—"namely that the dependent countries lack an autonomous capacity for development (cannot expand through self-impulsion) is shared by most dependencistas."[75] Their central belief is that an initial stature of dependence limits a nation's range of choice in pursuit of its desired mix of development goals. Thus, dependency obtains despite economic growth, ultimately denying the upper limits of development, and thereby mitigating against eventual entry into the club of advanced, interdependent capitalist states. While these dependency writers concede instances of waxing political and economic autonomy in dependent LDCs, they submit that fluctuations are limited in degree and of a cyclical nature, rather than "secular and progressive"[76] and, thereby, have no lasting effect on the underlying, encompassing and impervious relationship of dependence.

This position places primary focus on the development goal of autonomy. In so doing, the arena of fertile discourse between dependency theory and modernization theory is circumscribed, being limited to a consideration of the possibility for *self-directed* development within a liberal, capitalist framework.

This work is designed with the above focus—constituting a study of some mechanisms of capitalist-guided dependency reversal.

To effect dependency reversal while progressing concurrently with economic growth and equitable wealth distribution will necessitate the gradual replacement of foreign control and dominance with competent and dynamic indigenous capacity. Thus, growth of the indigenous entrepreneurial sector is requisite.

Modernization theory contends that the growth of indigenous business will be a consequence of the transformation of traditional societal structures, including a more liberal receptiveness to international capitalism. On the other hand, dependency theory denies the possibility for the emergence and sustained growth of a successful indigenous entrepreneurial class in the dependent capitalist state, precluding increased self-reliance and self-direction—necessary components for dependency reversal.

In their mutual attention to indigenous entrepreneurship in the dependent state, the competing theories provide a common variable against which their theoretical positions on the multinational corporation and dependency reversal may be evaluated. The rationale for this focus is reinforced in the following chapter, where the prominence of entrepreneurship as a key causal agent of development is substantiated.

CHAPTER 2

Entrepreneurship and Development

The role of the entrepreneur in economic progress was rarely addressed by 19th-century economists, who denied the entrepreneur a position among the three recognized factors of production: land, labor, and capital.

Arthur H. Cole, founding chairman of Harvard University's Research Center in Entrepreneurial History,[1] described in 1946 how the economic mainstream had continued to neglect entrepreneurship, attributing the oversight to its analytical frame of reference: "Economists since Ricardo have been largely preoccupied with 'long-run' conditions, 'static' analysis, and the like, and thereby have tended to distract attention from the short-run, but repetitive, forces that are productive."[2]

In the "long run," the entrepreneur's function of organizing the factors of production was taken for granted. Thus, as Mark Casson notes in *The Entrepreneur: An Economic Theory,* "decision-making [was] trivialized, reducing it to the mechanical application of mathematical rules for optimization."[3]

Many economists did concede the significance of the entrepreneurial function; however, Peter Kilby claims that of those who did, most relegated it "to the lower realms, where imperfect knowledge and market failure are granted an untidy presence."[4] Kilby asserts that the neglect of entrepreneurship by contemporary economists is not as thorough but still is the prevailing tendency of the orthodox mainstream:

> The economist who operates in the mainstream of his discipline assumes that the supply of entrepreneurial services is highly elastic and that failures in entrepreneurship are attributable to maladjustments in the external environment. Thus, the determinants of entrepreneurial performance lie on the demand side, in the structure of economic incentives—the home ground of the economist.[5]

27

By this treatment, the entrepreneur assumes only incidental status, serving merely to restore and maintain market equilibrium—by reflexive, rational responses to clear economic signals, an activity for which a sufficient and capable supply of entrepreneurs is presumed to be available.

The conceptualization of entrepreneurship as a causal agent in economic growth did not gain wide regard until after World War II, with the emergence of modernization theory and its attempt to reverse Third World stagnation (see Chapter 1). Leading theorists of the modernization school regard the entrepreneur as a central factor in development. For their purposes, the relevant segment of entrepreneurs is that connected with industry—manufacturing, service, or agribusiness. It is the expansion of this segment that is believed to hold the greatest promise for sustained LDC development. Therefore, small, low-growth, traditional operations such as "mom-and-pop" grocery stores, "market women," and street vendors, although entrepreneurial by nature and function, are typically not considered to be part of the development vanguard. This convention—restricting the focus to the entrepreneur who operates in the modern industrial or service sectors—shall henceforth be implicit in the discussion of the entrepreneur.

Modern entrepreneurial theory recalls the early-19th-century work of Jean Baptiste Say. Say claimed that it was the entrepreneur who

> "unites all means of production—the labor of the one, the capital or the land of others—and who finds the value of the products which result from their employment the reconstitution of the entire capital that he utilizes, and the value of the wages, the interest, and the rent which he pays, as well as the profit belonging to himself."[6]

Furthermore, Say viewed the entrepreneur as possessing special qualities:

> judgement, perseverance, and a knowledge of the world as well as of business. He is called upon to estimate with tolerable accuracy, the importance of a specific product, the probable amount of the demand, and the means of its production; at one time, he must employ a great number of hands; at another, buy or order the raw material, collect laborers, find consumers, and give at all times a rigid attention to order and economy; in a word, he must possess the art of superintendence and administration. . . . In the course of such complex operations, there

are an abundance of obstacles to be surmounted, of anxieties to be repressed, of misfortunes to be repaired, and of expedients to be devised.[7]

For more than 100 years after Say, the significance of the entrepreneur was largely overlooked, until Joseph Schumpeter, the eminent Austrian economist, designated the entrepreneur as the spearhead of economic development.[8] In Schumpeter's writings, the major role of the entrepreneur was as an innovator, through the introduction of new products, ideas, or services to the marketplace. Schumpeter's entrepreneur was a unique creature, a "captain of industry" distinguishable from from the typical owner, inventor, or business manager. To Schumpeter, entrepreneurs were heroic figures, who served to forestall the decay in capitalism that his classical predecessors had foreseen. Basically, Schumpeter describes innovation of a non-trivial, non-incremental nature. His entrepreneur is seen as an innovator of a special kind, introducing products and ideas that are revolutionary, which thereby create the discontinuous surges in progress that he perceived to be characteristic of capitalist development:

> Development in our sense is a distinct phenomenon, entirely foreign to what may be observed in the circular flow or in the tendency toward equilibrium. It is spontaneous and discontinuous change in the channel of the flow, disturbance of equilibrium, which forever alters and displaces the equilibrium state previously existing. . . . The author begs to add another more exact definition. . . . [Development] is that kind of change arising from within the system which so displaces its equilibrium point that the new one cannot be reached from the old one by infinitesimal steps.[9]

Schumpeter's idea of the entrepreneur as being one among a select few has been considered too restrictive by succeeding theorists. Nevertheless, Schumpeter's influence in the field has been profound. Indeed, since Schumpeter, the innovative function of the entrepreneur has been given a central position in the study of development.

Schumpeter no doubt was referring to entrepreneurs from developed countries in his writings, thereby excluding the Third World, where modest innovations represented in smaller business combinations are the rule. In contrast, subsequent theories of entrepreneurship have been more embracing, including virtually all those who initiate a business enterprise, irrespective of size.

Idiosyncratically, Schumpeter also declared that entrepreneurship was a function distinct from management and claimed that the entrepreneur actually ceased to exist once the routine of daily business management had replaced the more innovative, early stages of business growth: "Everyone is an entrepreneur only when he actually 'carries out new combinations,' and loses that character as soon as he has built up his business, when he settles down to running it as other people run their businesses."[10]

In contrast, most contemporary writers consider the owner-manager of a business to be an entrepreneur.[11] This perspective broadens the entrepreneurial role by according equal status to the managerial function in recognition of the special skills that are required for successful and ongoing enterprise. As Benjamin Higgins describes:

> He is a man who sees the opportunity for introducing the new commodity, technique, raw material, or machine, and brings together the necessary capital, management, labor, and materials to do it. He may not be, and historically has usually not been, a scientific inventor. His skills are less scientific than organizational. His skills are also different from those of a salaried manager, who takes over an enterprise after it has been launched. In any society, the rate of technological progress and so of economic development depends greatly on the number and the ability of entrepreneurs available to it.[12]

For purposes of summary, a conventional definition of the entrepreneur is offered from the *Random House Dictionary of the English Language,* 2d ed. (1987): "A person who organizes and manages any enterprise, especially a business, usually with considerable initiative and risk."

Since World War II, modernization theories have recognized the role of the entrepreneur in introducing the changes necessary to advance Third World countries from stagnation. For example, W. Arthur Lewis has stated that the process of economic development "is bound to be slow unless there is an adequate supply of entrepreneurs looking out for new ideas, and willing to take the risk of introducing them."[13] Similarly, A. O. Hirschman describes the importance of entrepreneurship, claiming that for LDCs, "their difficulty . . . lies . . . with the perception of investment opportunities and their transformation into actual investment."[14]

The public sector has also accorded paramount importance to entrepreneurship in the furthering of development. For example, in his presidential address to the Board of Governors of the World Bank,

Robert S. McNamara stated: "Economic development requires financial resources. Indeed, it requires far more than have yet been made available. But the resource it requires most is creative innovation."[15]

After World War II, development theories initially gave entrepreneurship and capital equal billing as causal agents of development;[16] however, Robert Buchele notes that a number of studies in the last 20 years have cited a growing trend in the literature of identifying entrepreneurship "as the key factor among a complex of interrelated factors such as the availability of capital, technological knowledge, natural resources, governmental organization, attitudes and motives."[17]

The recent focus upon entrepreneurship as *the* key development factor may be attributed to evidence from certain LDCs that capital is not lacking, contrary to previous supposition. For example, in Nigeria there is general agreement by outside observers that a shortage of capital is not a major problem, even though it is perceived to be so by indigenous businessmen themselves.[18] Hirschman attempts to account for frequent misperceptions of low capital availability in LDCs (generally inferred from low savings levels), noting that "savings may be low because investments are low rather than vice-versa."[19] Thus, Hirschman is suggesting that there may be a "supply" problem in LDCs, reflecting a shortage of entrepreneurs capable of motivating additional savings from the local population. Accordingly, it may be argued "that, in a capitalist economy, the demand for capital funds often creates its own supply."[20]

That entrepreneurship is the preeminent factor in development may be disputed; nevertheless, its noted scarcity among LDCs with seemingly abundant supplies of land, labor, and capital prompts the conclusion that entrepreneurship is certainly a central factor in development, justifying the study of its nature and causes.

The three goals of development—economic growth, income equality, and autonomy[21]—are each enhanced by increases in entrepreneurial activity. Through initiating business ventures, successful entrepreneurs create new economic value, thereby increasing GNP growth and provoking income distribution through creating additional jobs. Furthermore, indigenous entrepreneurship contributes to the expansion of local autonomy and self-reliance, leading to lessened foreign dependence.

Given the prominence of the entrepreneurial function, an attempt to identify the entrepreneurial character is relevant, aiming to isolate the particular personality traits and sociological determinants that might distinguish the potential entrepreneur. Successful description of the entrepreneurial character would thereby facilitate the identification of potential entrepreneurs within a population. Consequently, government could devise cost-efficient development policy (e.g., training programs, advanced educational opportunities, subsidized loans, etc.) to target directly the designated, would-be entrepreneurs.

There are many and varied descriptions of the entrepreneurial character. Next the more noteworthy will be critically evaluated.

Max Weber, the eminent German sociologist, claimed that the Protestant Ethic was the driving force behind capitalist growth, prompting individuals to apply themselves assiduously to the rigors of business enterprise.[22] Weber viewed the Protestant Ethic as having liberated the entrepreneur from the institutional, cultural, and psychological barriers to personal initiative that Catholic tradition had erected and maintained.

While the Protestant Ethic can plausibly explain Western European industrial expansion, its general application falls short when having to account for entrepreneurship in modern Japan, for example, or in other developed countries of non-Protestant culture. Failure in this regard makes the role of Protestantism as a force motivating economic growth in Western Europe itself less plausible, suggesting that other, more universal factors may possess greater explanatory power.

David McClelland, a psychologist, accepted Weber's thesis regarding the presence of traditional barriers to entrepreneurship, but observed as others had that non-Protestant societies have produced many innovating individuals who display traits similar to Weber's Protestant entrepreneur. McClelland conducted extensive comparative research in attempting to determine the causes for the relative abundance or absence of entrepreneurs among various societies, evaluating the personal motives of the entrepreneur. Based on his findings, McClelland concluded that "a society with a high level of n Achievement [i.e., need for achievement] will produce more energetic entrepreneurs who, in turn, produce more rapid economic development."[23]

McClelland advises that governments attempting to forward the development process should attempt to "(1) break orientation toward tradition and increase other-directedness ... (2) increase n Achievement, and (3) provide for better allocation of existing n Achievement resources."[24]

Despite a chorus of early praise for McClelland's work,[25] later criticism has provided compelling evidence that his conclusions were unjustified. For example, Peter Kilby has noted that McClelland did not actually correlate *n* Achievement (measured through fantasy story scores) with economic growth.[26] Instead, another "independent" variable (achievement imagery in primary school textbooks) was utilized for experimental purposes. Ironically, achievement imagery actually proved to be *negatively* correlated with economic growth. Based upon this result, a straightforward conclusion would have been that high need for achievement does not explain economic growth (or that it leads to economic decline). However, in a "flip-flop" reminiscent of Freud, McClelland explained that high achievement imagery found in textbooks of poorer LDCs was a behavioral reaction against the low achievement motivation that actually prevailed in the society, allowing him to sustain his conclusion that high need for achievement motivates economic development. As McClelland rationalizes: "It is as if many of the backward countries realize their backwardness and are now motivated to close the gap between themselves and the more industrially developed countries. Such an interpretation will surprise no-one."[27]

In addition, McClelland's choice of indicator for describing the dependent variable (economic growth) has been strongly criticized. Sayre Schatz faults McClelland for failing to utilize growth of national product as the best index of economic growth.

> McClelland finds reason for rejecting national product in favor of the generation of electricity. While electrical output is sometimes used as one indicator of growth, it may not be coincidental that in McClelland's data *n* Achievement has a much higher correlation with the growth of kilowatt hours (.53) than with the growth of national product (.25). Particularly in view of the fact that in an earlier essay McClelland accepted income as the best measure of economic growth, one may be permitted to suspect that his choice might have been different if the correlations were reverse.[28]

These criticisms are truly severe, but perhaps more pertinent to the search for the entrepreneurial character is McClelland's failure to utilize a common definition of the entrepreneur.

> I am not using the term "entrepreneur" in any sense of "capitalist": In fact, I should like to divorce "entrepreneur" entirely from any connotations of ownership. An entrepreneur is someone who exercises

control over production that is not just for his personal consumption. According to my definition, for example, an executive in a steel-production unit in the U.S.S.R. is an entrepreneur.[29]

Thus, McClelland does not distinguish between the employee-manager and the owner-manager in his definition and, therefore, does not contribute to the present endeavor—that is, of separately identifying the innovative and dynamic entrepreneurial character.

Nevertheless, McClelland's theory of entrepreneurship is frequently cited in the literature and, in fact, has spawned numerous entrepreneurship programs. In these programs, "potential" entrepreneurs are given achievement motivation training (supplemented by various other forms of assistance) to help liberate untapped entrepreneurial capacity. It is difficult to assess the results of these programs, but of those that claim to be successful (indeed, many do not), the highly interpretive nature of their results has provoked considerable challenge.[30] In any case, whatever the true success rate of "McClelland-type" entrepreneurial training, the weakness of his supporting research leads the skeptical to look elsewhere for the latent entrepreneur, who might reasonably be presumed capable of superior business achievement when compared with McClelland's "n Achiever."

Everett E. Hagen, writing in 1962 as a contemporary of McClelland, similarly advanced a psychological (and also sociological) theory of entrepreneurship. In Hagen's observations, certain hard-driving, creative personalities were found in relatively high proportion among elite minority groups whose ancestors, many generations earlier, had experienced a "withdrawal of status respect" by the dominant elite of their society. The creative personality is said to have developed through an intergenerational sequence of personality changes stimulated by the earlier status withdrawal. When creative individuals from this subdominant elite are discriminated against, Hagen noted a relatively high tendency among them to compensate for their social frustration through the initiation of business ventures. Hagen provided examples from Russia, Japan, and Colombia, where Old Believers, Samurai, and Antioquinas, respectively, experienced status withdrawal in the 16th and 17th centuries. Hagen claimed that a disproportionate number of descendants from these groups were leaders in economic development, via innovative business formations. Hagen theorized that social rejection served to loosen traditional cultural constraints to initiative, facilitating the adoption of modern values and traits that complement the entrepreneurial function. He summarizes:

> Thus, I suggest, there gradually emerges a group of individuals, creative, alienated from traditional values, driven by a gnawing, burning drive to prove themselves (to themselves as well as to their fellows), seeking for an area in which to do so, preferably an area in which they can gain power and preferably one in which in some symbolic way they can vent their rage at the elites who have caused their troubles. Moreover, their (perhaps unconscious) rage at the group disparaging them will cause them to turn against some of the values of the group disparaging them. The fact that the disparaging group [in cases cited], was traditional, is one of the reasons why the disparaged group rejected traditional values and turned toward innovation.[31]

Hagen argued that the leaders of development always arise from a subdominant group seeking to compensate grievances through engaging in entrepreneurial activity.[32] Disputing Hagen's assertion, studies from Argentina[33] and Sweden[34] show that entrepreneurs from the *dominant* elite were almost wholly responsible for driving late-19th-century and early-20th-century development. In addition, contrary but equally plausible explanations for Hagen's own data have been offered. For example, William Long has claimed that the emergence of coffee growing in Antioquia from the early 1880s is virtually the entire cause of the development pattern described by Hagen, due to the Antioquinas having the best soils in Colombia rather than extraordinary entrepreneurial predispositions.[35]

McClelland and Hagen garnered swift interest and acceptance for their theories of entrepreneurship. Their studies, alongside Weber's *The Protestant Ethic and Spirit of Capitalism,* still rank as the most extensively cited in the literature. Nevertheless, their early support rapidly dissipated, burdened by the accumulating weight of contrary evidence. In addition, less prominent, competing theories were able to fare no better against critical scrutiny, accounting for the current lack of consensus regarding the entrepreneurial personality. In describing this scholarly frustration, Peter Kilby has likened the search for the elusive entrepreneurial personality to the futile hunt for the fictional "Heffalump" of "Winnie-The-Pooh" literature.[36]

As early as the mid-1960s, scholars forged a new direction in entrepreneurial research. Their approach dispensed with the quest to designate the psychological traits that might distinguish the entrepreneurial personality. In these recent schemes, the entrepreneur is regarded as being the product of the surrounding set of opportunities rather than a behavioral manifestation of a unique personality type. Sidney Greenfield describes this approach in summarizing the work of William P. Glade, who argued that what had distinguished entrepreneurial behavior

> were the settings, circumstances, or situations within which the choices were made. These he termed "opportunity structures." As these exogenous factors changed, they provided new opportunities for members of a society. In their decisions and choices, some might take advantage of the new opportunities while others did not. Those who did, and were successful, came to be called entrepreneurs; they broke old equilibrium and moved economy and society to new ones.[37]

This framework can be utilized to account for failures to identify the "entrepreneurial personality." In fact, like Pooh's imaginary Heffalump, a distinctive entrepreneurial personality may indeed not exist. In any case, given continuing frustration with personality research, Glade's "opportunity structure" would appear to provide a more promising alternative. Thus, in presuming an inability to identify the entrepreneurial personality, social policies or "institutional arrangements" designed to promote a "desirable" opportunity structure are expected to maximize entrepreneurial initiative and success in business. Bert Hoselitz, writing prior to McClelland and Hagen, counseled a similar policy orientation for underdeveloped countries interested in promoting entrepreneurship:

> Since it is impossible for a centralized agency to plan effectively for the kind of personality orientation which is to prevail, the only freedom left for planners who favor a particular set of actions is to create external conditions which will attract individuals with appropriate orientations to engage in certain roles designed to lead to the desired objective. In more concrete terms, if social planning in underdeveloped countries is directed toward stimulating the evolution of free industrial entrepreneurship, it must provide for the establishment of external, objective conditions which will make such entrepreneurial behavior an attractive or even strongly approved alternative of social behavior.[38]

Thus, without identifying the potential entrepreneur, Hoselitz asserts that public policy broadly oriented toward competitive, free-market principles will serve to create the ideal opportunity structure for entrepreneurship in the LDC. Consonant with the institutionalist perspective of modernization theory, Hoselitz also acknowledges the utility of supplementing such policy with positive institutional arrangements designed to specifically motivate entrepreneurial activity.

Harvey Liebenstein, an economist, similarly concluded that the availability of economic opportunity is one of the critical variables conditioning the "actual employment of entrepreneurial skills in an economy."[39] Liebenstein, however, differs from Hoselitz in that he views enhanced opportunity structures as insufficient to remedy depressed entrepreneurial activity in the less developed world. Liebenstein, in fact, would perceive no dearth of opportunity in the less developed world, seeing opportunity as generally available to the insightful entrepreneur who gains the knowledge necessary to exploit the LDC's characteristic and widespread market inefficiencies. In the less developed world, Leibenstein asserted that these inefficiencies are the rule among indigenously owned businesses, being unable to maximize their production functions and operating at an "X-efficiency" far short of optimization.[40] Liebenstein sees entrepreneurs as the key individuals in developing society, acquiring information that is domestically scarce and bridging market gaps in the "obstructed, incomplete, and 'relatively dark' economic systems"[41] in which they operate.

Liebenstein felt that entrepreneurs in the developing world, unfortunately, were too few in number and insufficiently skilled to respond with suitable alacrity to expanded economic opportunity. Thus, Liebenstein did not perceive "neoclassical, free market" solutions to be adequate for stimulating the level of entrepreneurial activity needed to increase X-efficiency among less developed countries. Alternatively, Liebenstein suggested that government might have a more expanded role in facilitating private entrepreneurship:

> For purposes of economic development it seems reasonable to presume that there may be a fairly large supply of gap filling skills but a very much smaller supply of input completing skills. Where this is the case, avenues may be opened for governmental intervention to influence the supply of entrepreneurship. For example, where the missing input completing skill is the provision of finance, the government creation of institutions which foster saving, capital accumulation, and the allocation of capital to users may increase input-completing skills for those who are currently gap fillers.[42]

Nevertheless, despite Liebenstein's willingness to diverge from standard neoclassical solutions, his counsel for government intervention is guarded, offered to refine rather than to supplant a general environment of free market institutional arrangements.

Israel Kirzner, also an economist, punctuates the importance Liebenstein gives to information, claiming that alertness to scarce information is the essential entrepreneurial talent,[43] enabling the bearer to take advantage of profit opportunities that derive from market inefficiencies and other sources of economic disequilibria. Kirzner, however, is more optimistic than Liebenstein that free market solutions will bring about the necessary levels of entrepreneurship in developing societies. In this respect, Kirzner claims that market oriented economies are best at motivating entrepreneurial alertness to new information, through providing superior profit opportunities:

> The social significance of a market system ... rests upon the capacity of markets to translate the error made in the immediate past into opportunities for pure entrepreneurial profit of direct interest to potential entrepreneurs. Features of the institutional landscape that strengthen the linkage between socially significant opportunities and the likelihood and security of associated entrepreneurial gain clearly improve the chances for entrepreneurial discovery.[44]

Together, Hoselitz, Liebenstein, and Kirzner share a position which generally regards a liberal, market-oriented economy to be superior in engendering successful entrepreneurial activity, although Liebenstein differs in suggesting that it is often preferable to diverge from this prescription, by creating public initiatives and ventures in cases where private enterprise is found to be lacking.

Strongly counterpoised, dependency theorists claim that a "free-market" orientation reinforces exploitative capitalism, perpetuating current dependent relationships and underdevelopment. A prominent consequence is claimed to be the inhibition of indigenous entrepreneurship. In this respect, the subsidiaries of multinational corporations from the advanced countries are viewed as the primary culprit, preventing the emergence of competing indigenous entrepreneurs through their monopolization and dominance of local industrial, capital, and labor markets.

The modernization perspective holds the opposite view, supporting a general orientation toward free market principles. To modernization theory, the MNC subsidiary serves as the primary modernizing agent and promoter of LDC development, and, therefore, is a critical element of the ideal opportunity structure, transferring technology, creating jobs, training managers, transmitting modern business culture, and forging supportive commercial linkages with indigenous business. Alternatively, lacking indigenous entrepreneurship is blamed on traditional and inefficient attitudes, institutions, and policies of the host state that depress economic incentive and business initiative.

Thus, an assessment of the developing state's and the MNC subsidiary's influence upon indigenous entrepreneurship presents the opportunity to evaluate the validity of parallel, competing claims that are *central* to the modernization and dependency theories of development.

CHAPTER 3

The State, the Multinational Corporation, and Entrepreneurship

With the brisk economic growth enjoyed by much of the Third World during the 1960s and 1970s, public policy was little concerned with eliminating the recognized shortage of entrepreneurs. Alternatively, state owned and controlled enterprises expanded their scope,[1] aiming to substitute for lack of private initiative. The record of state enterprise, however, was dismal. Typically mismanaged, corrupt, and unprofitable, public enterprises are today being privatized in ever increasing numbers. Consequently, public attention is being reoriented to focus upon the continuing undersupply of Third World entrepreneurs, adopting the view that Third World entrepreneurial ranks must enlarge in order to reverse the prolonged economic stagnation of the past decade.[2]

The State and Entrepreneurship

Relative to the identified shortage of indigenous industrial entrepreneurship in the Third World, the role of the state occupies a central position in both modernization theory and dependency theory. Modernization theory lays blame for lack of entrepreneurship and underdevelopment on the traditional attitudes, culture, and institutions of the LDC, viewing them to be incompatible with economic progress.

In considering the historical record, traditional attitudes and cultures have not proven to be uniformly prohibitive of entrepreneurship and development. For instance, the Confucian Ethic was a cultural attitude often ascribed to Asian societies by Westerners in accounting for their underdevelopment and the perceived disdain of Asians to initiate and toil in industrial enterprise (in contrast to the Protestant Ethic). In recent years, however, vigorous entrepreneurial activity combined with strong and sustained growth in Japan and in the newly industrialized countries of the Far East has decisively shattered this cultural and attitudinal stereotype. Likewise, in Latin America, traditional attitudes and culture of Iberian origin have long been held responsible for continued underdevelopment, yet Latin America's progenitors—Spain and Portugal—are today among the developed, industrial ranks of the European Economic Community, while Brazil and Mexico, despite their numerous difficulties, are 10th and 12th, respectively, in terms of GDP among industrialized countries.[3]

In many developing countries, entrepreneurship in the traditional, informal sector abounds; however, sustained modern development requires the emergence and growth of an *industrial* entrepreneurial corps, a group lacking in membership in the Third World.

As traditional culture, attitudes, and robust industrial development may coexist, a narrowing of the modernization perspective's focus toward institutional factors may provide a better explanation of the lack of LDC industrial entrepreneurship. Also important, institutionally oriented policy adjustments would likely prove less socially disruptive than attempted cultural overhaul.

Egypt provides a good example of institutional backwardness. In Egypt, commercial incentives have been eroded through government intervention in the marketplace. Government bureaucracies assert broad control over pricing and are active in selectively subsidizing favored industries. Furthermore, as Elias Tuma explains, planning is difficult because these controls are arbitrarily applied, unevenly enforced, and often quickly changed, raising the risk level associated with doing business.

> Those who consider the government policy on price and subsidy as favorable cannot be certain that the policy will last very long and therefore hesitate to make long-term plans on its basis; and those who regard that policy as unfavorable also hesitate, with the hope that the policy will change to a more positive one in the near future. In either case, indecision and procrastination follow so as to avoid being caught off guard when the change comes.[4]

Industrial entrepreneurship can not thrive in such an environment, for a long-term perspective is required in order to motivate requisite large, up-front investment. Tuma argues the opposite environment prevails in Egypt: "The indecision and lax enforcement . . .

encourage a rush for quick benefits, while the opportunity prevails. If caught in the process, one tries to escape enforcement of the laws through personal contacts and informal favors."[5]

Dependency theorists claim that such corruption and associated institutional inefficiencies are symptomatic of an LDC's enmeshment in the international capitalist system. Dependency theory diminishes the autonomous role of the state in developing societies; therefore, successful institutional overhaul along free market, capitalist lines is not seen as an available reform; it is disallowed by external parties who favor the status quo. Socialist revolution is the preferred solution; however, dependencistas' more pragmatic and immediate reforms target the MNC subsidary, aiming to constrict its magnitude and scope in the LDC economy. The MNC is blamed to be the critical external element in a dependence maintaining alliance with local capital from both private and state-controlled sources.[6] Together, these parties are claimed to condition the direction and extent of industrialization through their influence over domestic political and economic institutions. Thus, dependencistas are critical of the institutionalist perspective, claiming that it ignores the MNC's responsibility for, and interest in, perpetuating dependence. To dependency theory, backward institutional structures and arrangements are only susceptible to change through restricting the MNC. But, as Peter Evans observes, dependencistas consider this difficult to achieve in the absence of socialist revolution, for those elements in the state apparatus who are nationalistically oriented

> are constrained by the necessity of fostering the enthusiasm of both the multinationals and local capitalists, constrained in a way that makes it extremely difficult to adopt a developmental strategy that would spread the benefits of industrialization more widely. Even if there is substantial support within the state apparatus for more welfare oriented policies, adopting such policies would threaten the whole elite consensus on which industrialization itself is based.[7]

Thus, in typical cases, the goals of autonomy and greater economic equality are sacrificed to capitalist industrialization. According to dependency theory, economic growth may proceed but largely to the benefit of a "triple alliance" consisting of the MNCs, state enterprises, and the local capitalist elite. This association enforces self-serving institutional arrangements for its constituent members while diminishing commercial incentive to potential entrepreneurs outside its sphere. Within the triple alliance, local entrepreneurs often flourish, as is strikingly demonstrated in cases of commercial partnerships with the MNC. But in aligning with foreign interests, these local entrepreneurs are no longer the champions of national development. By relying upon foreign technology and state subsidy and preference, local entrepreneurship may thrive—but in a limited and dependent form. Dependency theorists characterize industrialization of this type as "dependent development," where "the rate and direction of accumulation are externally conditioned."[8] In this environment, autonomous indigenous business is inhibited by state policies which exclusively benefit members of the triple alliance. Through their favored positions, MNC subsidiaries, state enterprises, and dependent entrepreneurs thrive, even when operating inefficiently, and are allowed to pass along the associated costs to the LDC consumer.

Today, LDCs seeking to controvert a dependent status rarely initiate the drastic option of expropriating foreign assets, although in the 1960s and early 1970s the practice occurred with frequency. While the recent trend may reflect the fact that the most criticized MNC subsidiaries have already been nationalized, the experience of inefficient state substitute enterprises and lacking private indigenous capabilities suggests that LDCs have reconsidered the efficiency of previous nationalization policies. For example, Michael Shafer's analysis of the copper industry of Zaire and Zambia illustrates an important lesson of MNC expropriation. For both countries, Shafer has shown that their nationalization of MNC assets was a poor idea that led to a significant deterioration in the financial performance of their copper industries.[9] To Shafer, Zaire and Zambia are representative of LDCs with relatively weak states and "insufficient cadres of trained managers and technicians."[10] These deficiencies are claimed to prevent the nationalized industry from effectively functioning, no longer insulated by the MNC from many economic and political pressures of international and domestic origin. Shafer cites Zaire and Zambia as being close to the Third World norm, thereby offering a general caveat against Third World nationalization.[11]

A less radical attempt to promote greater national autonomy while preserving some of the benefits provided by the MNC is represented by the joint venture. Joint ventures between LDCs and MNCs from developed countries are often claimed to be ideal instruments for promoting the whole slate of LDC development goals. In considering the joint venture in Latin America, Wolfgang G. Friedman and George Kalmanoff state:

The less developed countries have come to see that cooperation with
industrially developed countries for the use of their capital, their resources, and their skills and experience is a more economic, and ultimately a quicker way of achieving industrialization than to "go it
alone." On the other hand, these countries have not abandoned the
basic ambition to attain national sovereignty, not only political but also
economic. This implies keeping control, or at least general direction,
over basic industries and, if possible, over the entire field of foreign
investment.[12]

Given the technical and managerial capabilities imparted to the
MNC-trained, joint venture workforce, the gradual emergence of an
indigenous cadre of industrial entrepreneurs is presumably facilitated.

In idealized form, joint ventures would appear to be the answer
to Third World underdevelopment and dependence, but in practice
their desirability is questionable. First of all, LDC joint venture laws
often mandate domestic majority control. A frequently noted example is Mexico, with its list of "critical" industries in which jointly
owned businesses must have at least 51 percent local ownership. This
arrangement is generally believed to inhibit a great deal of foreign
investment, due to the reluctance of prospective foreign investors to
yield control to less seasoned indigenous partners. Also, many foreign
investors are concerned with maintaining security over proprietary
technology. Thus, there is a fundamental tradeoff between attracting
foreign investment and maintaining stringent joint venture regulations. On the whole, the current trend is toward more liberal joint
venture policy. In Mexico, for example, the "51 percent rule" has
been relaxed for a number of industries, allowing 100 percent foreign
ownership for qualifying companies.

While joint venture mandates inhibit foreign investment flow,
those joint ventures that do occur are not regarded as wholly positive
with respect to Third World development goals. Joint ventures are
often criticized by dependency writers for providing foreign investors
with a means "(1) to gain the right to produce well known branded
products and (2) to gain a protector against local competition and
other foreign firms entering the market."[13] Through these competitive advantages, more extensive foreign dependence would presumably follow.

Through joint venture mandates, the host country receives concessions from the foreign investor in exchange for the right to invest
and do business. Of course, a joint venture requirement is but one of

the many strategies that a host country might adopt. Its success in exacting concessions from the MNC, whether through joint venture or by other means, is said to vary with its "bargaining strength." Over time, relative bargaining strength is claimed to increase for the host country, a tendency popularly referred to as the "obsolescing bargain":[14] "The dynamism in the obsolescing bargain that accounts for a shift in power from the foreign investor to the host country springs from the dissipation of risk and uncertainty if the project proves successful. It may also come from a kind of hostage effect, where the company cannot easily threaten to withdraw, credibly, once its investment has been sunk."[15]

In addition, the bargaining power of the host country can be augmented "as the country moves up a learning curve of bargaining and managerial skills, the better to drive a hard bargain with the foreigner and/or to threaten to replace him if he balks at renegotiating the successful contract."[16]

Shafer's analysis of the copper industry of Zaire and Zambia reinforces the importance of this latter source of bargaining power. While acknowledging that incremental concessions from the international copper industry were available, Shafer asserts that there was insufficient indigenous capability to press for the goal of full nationalization—thus explaining the failure.

Similarly, Gary Gereffi has described in a study of the international pharmaceutical industry in Mexico how bargaining power is primarily limited by the ability of the host country to "duplicate many of the technological and managerial capabilities of the multinationals."[17]

According to modernization theory, the development of indigenous capacity to counter foreign dominance is a natural consequence of diffusion from the local MNC subsidiary, transmitted through indigenous managers, suppliers, and competitors. On the other hand, advocates of a bargaining strategy are less patient. While acknowledging the positive features of a moderate foreign presence in industry, they advocate state intervention in directing local resources to counteract MNC dominance, thereby reducing foreign dependence. Thus, the bargaining school steers a middle course between the more liberal institutionalists of the modernization perspective and the more radical dependencistas, aiming to parlay benefit from foreign direct investment (fdi) into bargaining power—then utilized by the state to supplant MNC dominance and to replace it with indigenous substitute enterprise.

Bargaining theory's core assumptions may be criticized for "correspond[ing] closely to those made in conventional economics,"[18] thus ignoring the political dimensions which some argue may be more explanatory of the frequent outcomes which contradict the "rational" predictions of the bargaining model. To elaborate, the bargaining model assumes the existence of a "maximizing" government operating on behalf of national interests and having "the power to negotiate with a foreign company, come to an agreement with it, and then enforce the agreement."[19] Yet in the Third World, governments are often weak or, in other cases, do not act in consideration of the national interest, rendering bargaining strategies unfeasible or undesirable.

Despite the limitations of the bargaining model, however, it is widely recognized that developing states have proven increasingly effective in asserting control over the economic activity taking place within their borders, manifesting an increase in their relative power within the international system.

Evidence of the obsolescing bargain is most strong in the vertically integrated, extractive industries, where foreign investments are characterized by high risk, sunk costs, government learning, and oligopolistic rivalry.[20] In these industries, there is considerable agreement in the literature that the bargaining model applies, manifest over time as a shift in relative power to host countries.[21]

In the manufacturing industries, however, there is less agreement regarding developing countries' abilities to increase their bargaining position over time vis-a-vis foreign capital. Despite sector-specific variations, manufacturing industries are generally characterized by lower risk, lower sunk costs, less national salience, and higher technology than in extractive industries, giving the host country less leverage when attempting to exact additional economic concessions from foreign investors.[22]

In addition, bargaining strategy proponents often overlook enhancements in the relative power of foreign investors, achieved because they adopt investment strategies that reduce the deterioration of the original bargain. For example, strategies of international sourcing have been shown to enhance the ability of the parent corporation to avoid expropriation or equity losses.[23] In addition, foreign investors who initially agree to performance standards (e.g., local content and export requirements) have been found to be more resilient to nationalization.[24] Finally, recent data suggests that the selection of local private partners may lessen the vulnerability of foreign investment. For instance, one study showed that the foreign companies least likely to be nationalized in Mexico, Zambia, and South Korea were those including local private partners.[25] Often, MNC subsidiaries in LDC manufacturing industries may actually gain in relative bargaining power subsequent to initial investment and are sometimes able to improve their domestic political position by forging business alliances with local suppliers, distributors, and financial institutions.[26]

Of course, the MNCs' defensive strategies may encounter countervailing measures adopted by host governments. And Alfred Stepan predicts that future increases in multinational activity may "result in an increase rather than a decrease of the state's role in the management of the economy. There is also a very real possibility that the growth of multinationals will stimulate the appearance of multistate planning and bargaining organizations such as the Andean Pact and OPEC."[27]

The bargaining school offers Joseph Grieco's study of the Indian computer industry as evidence that state initiative can even gain concessions from international capital in the manufacturing industry and, meanwhile, successfully develop domestic industrial alternatives.[28] In India, the desire to develop national self-sufficiency in the manufacture of all but the largest and most exotic computer systems led to state demands upon major foreign operators for equity sharing. Burroughs and International Computer Limited acceded to India's demands in the late 1970s; however, IBM (the market leader[29]) decided to withdraw from the country. Grieco details the dramatic growth in domestic industry accompanying IBM's withdrawal from the Indian market.

Similarly, Emanuel Adler has shown how Brazilian state policy toward the multinationals in its computer industry enabled indigenous substitutes to flourish and expand:[30] "In June of 1977 ... the Brazilian government refused IBM, Burroughs, NCR and several other leading transnational corporations in the computer field permission to manufacture mini-computers in Brazil, choosing instead to stake its high technology future on five locally-owned firms, all of them small and recently formed."[31]

Brazilian policy was impressive in achieving a measure of autonomy for domestic enterprise:

> Between its inception in 1978 and 1982, the dollar sales of the domestic [computer] industry grew from 2 percent of the total to 19 percent. By 1982 domestic companies had produced 67 percent of

installed computers.... By 1983 one hundred Brazilian computer companies were employing eighteen thousand people, twelve hundred of them in research and development, and were generating annual sales of 687 million dollars.[32]

Grieco has claimed that the Third World activity of the international computer industry should provide an "easy case" for dependencistas to illustrate their theory's validity.[33] For example, Peter Evans, representing the dependency position, has "argued that transnational corporations would dominate industries where intangible capital (like proprietary technology and marketing expertise) is the key source of competitive advantage, especially if the industries were highly oligopolistic."[34] India's and Brazil's early computer industries would seem to fit into Evans's category of those industries that are most susceptible to MNC domination, thus leading Grieco to claim that the observed reversals in both Brazil's and India's computer industries provide strong argument against the general validity of dependency theory.

On the other hand, although the computer industries in both countries have been transformed, Evans counsels "that it would be foolish to try to deny the extent of Brazil's [continuing] dependence on international firms and international technology."[35] In any case, neither Adler nor Grieco has claimed that dependence in either country's computer industry has been overcome. At issue is the degree and significance of the advances in indigenous industrial development in light of national goals. While progress in domestic self-reliance is considered a vital goal of development, efficiency costs must not be ignored. Grieco and Adler largely avoid this consideration, presenting arguments that contend more directly with industry-specific dependency issues than with the broader context of development. Indeed, it is significant to note that both the Indian and Brazilian computer industries are presently characterized by inefficiency. The tradeoff between inefficiency costs and autonomy goals cannot be overlooked, as data processing and management information systems costs are significant components of industrial corporate balance sheets. Whereas an "infant industry" strategy can justify absorbing short term "autonomy" costs in favor of long term political and economic gains, protracted protectionism must overcome stagnationist tendencies. For example, in Brazil, interested parties had enough power to push legislation protecting the microcomputer industry; however, they never had enough power to link it with broader industrial and economic policies or with a long-range program of scientific and technological research. Instead they created a stalemate that ... intensified during the Sarney government and transformed the informatics policy from an aggressive project of technological self-reliance into a purely defensive screen for a group of stagnant and largely ineffective microcomputer assembly plants.[36]

In India, deficiencies of the insulated domestic computer industry led former prime minister Rajiv Gandhi to announce policy changes that reduce protectionism with the goal of modernizing the industry and making it more competitive internationally.[37] Yet despite recent Indian policies, great damage has already been done from years of "reinventing the wheel" rather than importing the latest foreign technology. Indian computer systems in place are considered antiquated and of low productive output, with similar systems having been introduced in the United States five to ten years earlier.[38] In addition, India's delay in rationalizing its computer policy has caused foreign businesses to invest elsewhere in the region.[39]

Of course, less cost conscious observers (i.e., the bargaining school) might contradict this indictment, judging in unabashedly positive terms the emergence of indigenous technological enterprise in Brazilian and Indian industries where MNCs once completely dominated.

As mentioned by members of the bargaining school, the indigenous availability of experienced technological and managerial personnel is a factor critical to the success of state policies seeking to erode MNC dominance. The most important among this indigenous corps would be entrepreneurs, who deliver the early impetus in the emergence of local industry and also provide a source of sustained dynamism over the longer term. For example, in the Indian computer case, government initiatives were at first unsuccessful in achieving their indigenization goals. Subsequently, however, the unexpected emergence of small but competitive (and unsubsidized) indigenous operations provided the necessary bargaining power for the initially successful effort to lessen foreign dependence and expand the market share of locally owned enterprise. It is interesting to note that of the four indigenous enterprises that Grieco cites as having catalyzed the success of Indian computer policy, one company, International Data Machines (IDM), was founded by former IBM employees.

Similarly, in Brazil, the gradual emergence of indigenous competition provided the stimulus for policymakers to proceed with plans
to restrict minicomputer production to domestically owned operations. Interestingly, Adler believes that most of the founding indigenous entrepreneurs of the major Brazilian computer firms had previous work experience with foreign owned MNCs[40]—the experience
presumably conferring upon them the skills to pursue independent
enterprise.

In addition to an abundant supply of indigenous technology and
managerial skills, Shafer and Gereffi highlight state and political
strength as essential for initiating, directing, and sustaining an accelerated drive for self-sufficiency in a particular industry. Furthermore,
Adler emphasizes that, besides political strength, the state must be
committed to an antidependency drive. For example, despite the fact
that Argentina has indigenous technological ability rivaling Brazil's,
and a strong and, until recently, interventionist government, its unsuccessful foray into computers in the 1970s was a case of what Adler
describes as "private initiative that failed to convince government of
its merits. . . . The difference lay in perceptions of development and
the existence of state institutions that could manage a project of technological self-reliance. The Brazilians focussed all along on reducing
dependency while the Argentines emphasized efficiency and the market."[41]

The scholarship of the bargaining school recognizes the need for
prior indigenous capabilities when a nation attempts to thwart MNC
dominance. Modernization theorists concur, but counsel state re-
straint in industrial policy, preferring to rely more heavily on private
indigenous initiative. Thus, they look favorably toward the emergence of indigenous entrepreneurs (many having previous MNC experience) in India's and Brazil's computer industry prior to forced
MNC retrenchment. To modernization theorists, these indigenous
entrepreneurs represent evidence of the "spread effect" of foreign
direct investment, making state intrusion into the computer industry
unwarranted.

On the other hand, dependency theorists have claimed that observed increases in indigenous skills are eventually appropriated by
the MNC, as it further extends its operations into LDC economies.
Successes in lessened dependency are claimed to be partial, not representing a fundamental trend toward balanced interdependence. No
less than the exclusion of the MNC from the LDC is claimed to be

necessary for bringing about vigorous and self-reliant indigenous entrepreneurship.

Supporters of the MNC argue that the quality of indigenous skill is positively enhanced through prolonged MNC exposure. Among these supporters, there is disagreement regarding the proper role of the state. The bargaining school is activist, regarding state intervention directed against the MNC as fundamental for eroding dependency. Nevertheless, the MNC is viewed in progressive terms, for it equips indigenous parties with the knowledge to bargain for advantage and to engage in substitute enterprise as the MNC is forced to retrench. Modernization theory, with its institutionalist perspective, is more liberal with respect to the proper role of the state. Above all, the state is expected to provide for an economy in which commercial incentives are safeguarded on a fair and competitive basis. State bias against the MNC and its protection of domestic players in favored industries is widely opposed by institutionalists, in accordance with their neoclassical roots. In their perspective, the promulgation of correct institutional arrangements (e.g., easy taxes, strongly supported intellectual and private property rights) will in time result in the emergence of local entrepreneurs to compete with the MNCs.

In summary, the decision of both dependency theory and the bargaining school to protect indigenous industry bases itself on a view that denies an overall benefit to the developing host country from a liberally constrained MNC.

Dependency critics of the MNC point to the recent vigorous growth and self-directedness enjoyed by several Southeast Asian economies in the absence of foreign industrial dominance, and thus they call for universal insulation from MNC investment. Similarly, proponents of the bargaining school cite state-directed indigenization in the Indian and Brazilian computer industry as reinforcing evidence for MNC containment.

In response, institutionalists dismiss the claim that low levels of fdi account for Southeast Asia's success, alternatively pointing to government policies differences in accounting for variable development progress among states (e.g., export led growth in Southeast Asia—an acknowledged success—versus import substitution industrialization in Latin America—a recognized failure). Institutionalists strongly support liberal fdi policies, praising the MNC for its special industrializing features and for its outstanding contribution to indigenous human capital.[42]

To rectify the acknowledged condition of lack of entrepreneurship in dependent countries, both dependency and modernization theorists concur that an overhaul of economic and political institutions must be undertaken. Their perspectives differ, however, due in large part to their opposing views regarding the effects of multinational investment upon entrepreneurship. With an aim to evaluate the contending perspectives on this dimension, a more detailed, systematic consideration of the effects of the foreign MNC subsidiary upon indigenous entrepreneurship in dependent host countries follows, resulting in the generation of hypotheses for subsequent empirical evaluation.

The Multinational Corporation and Entrepreneurship

With respect to Third World entrepreneurship, both theories of development attach central importance to the role of the MNC subsidiary, whether as an inhibitor (dependency theory) or a catalyst (modernization theory).

In order to justify the theoretical prominence given to the MNC in its influence upon Third World entrepreneurship, an initial review of the MNC's financial and commercial breadth is presented.

The subsidiary of the multinational corporation is the major vehicle for foreign equity investment in the Third World. As of 1981, the developed countries had amassed a stock of direct investment in the developing countries in excess of $131 billion, with the United States accounting for 48 percent of the total.[43] Yet despite the large sum, the relative magnitude is small compared to the total of LDC capital stock. For instance, in Mexico, the second largest recipient of foreign direct investment in the developing world,[44] foreign investment is estimated to comprise only 4.3% of all productive investment.[45] Furthermore, it is estimated that MNC employment accounts for only 0.5 percent of the total labor force of the underdeveloped countries of Africa, Asia, and Latin America.[46] Nevertheless, these broad statistics lead to an underestimation of the great impact that MNCs have upon many individual developing countries. Looking more closely, MNC subsidiaries tend to be concentrated among the wealthier of LDCs. In fact, 58 percent of fdi is concentrated in only 14 of 132 developing countries,[47] while Mexico and Brazil alone account for more than 20 percent of total fdi in developing countries.[48]

In Latin America today, and similarly worldwide, a majority of fdi is concentrated in manufacturing (with a small but increasing share in services), a statistic attributable to the decreased role of the MNC in primary (extractive and agricultural) sectors. This shift has proceeded from expropriations and exclusions of MNCs in the primary sector of developing countries, in part due to their operations being "connected" to the land and, thereby, viscerally associated with diminished host sovereignty.[49] On the other hand, host governments often have been active in seeking fdi in manufacturing, offering a variety of financial incentives (e.g., tax holidays, tariff barriers, etc.) in accord with import substitution industrialization policies. The extent of MNC concentration in Latin America is indeed pronounced. As of 1970, foreign MNCs accounted for 20 percent of Brazil's manufacturing employment, 28 percent of Argentina's, and 28 percent of Colombia's.[50] In Mexico, foreign MNCs accounted for 21 percent of manufacturing employment,[51] and a much larger 35 to 40 percent of total manufacturing investment.[52] Furthermore, 84 percent of Mexico's foreign investment is in industries in which the combined market share of the four largest firms exceeds 50 percent of the market,[53] creating high visibility for MNCs in these industries. Mexico's experience is typical of LDCs with relatively high fdi stocks.

Logically, the manufacturing sector is considered the most crucial for early industrializing countries; thus, high MNC concentration in the sector evokes great concern regarding the national goal of self-reliant development. This concern is given support by dependency theory. To the dependencistas, the MNC subsidiary serves as the nexus for a dependence maintaining alliance of domestic elites with foreign capital. Theotonio dos Santos describes the resulting system as "a dependent one because it reproduces a productive system whose development is limited to those world relations which necessarily lead to the development of only certain economic sectors, to trade under unequal conditions, to the imposition of relations of super-exploitation of the labor force with a view to dividing the economic surplus between the internal and external forces of exploitation."[54]

In contrast, modernization theory regards the MNC subsidiary favorably. MNCs are viewed as importing resources in scarce supply locally (e.g., capital, technology, managerial and marketing skills), stimulating efficiency, adding jobs, and even improving income distribution (by lowering the returns to capital while bidding up wages).[55] In fact, Peter Drucker claims that many perceive MNCs to be "the only real hope" for LDCs,[56] attributing to them additional progressive features: "[MNCs alter] traditional value systems, social attitudes, and behavior patterns, and they encourage responsibility among the political leadership of less-developed countries. By improving the economic situation and capabilities of less-developed countries, multinationals facilitate political development."[57]

Although they draw opposite conclusions, both modernization and dependency theorists regard MNC activity as a leading indicator of development. For modernization theory, the MNC offers to lead the LDCs in shedding their outmoded structures, stimulating the development of a modern, industrial culture and fostering an internal dynamism that will eventually lessen vulnerability to advanced economies, to achieve a more symmetric and self-reliant form of interdependence. For dependency theory, development will be hastened only as the exploitative capacity of the MNC is neutralized, a first step toward more autonomous and less vulnerable national development.

Thus, for both perspectives, lessened economic vulnerability, greater self-reliance, and enhanced development are expected to grow along with indigenously initiated enterprise. In this respect, both modernization and dependency theorists see the entrepreneur as at the vanguard of heightened development. Dependencistas would argue that Third World entrepreneurs would bring about the coming of the millennium if not for MNC penetration.[58] In contrast, according to modernization theory, the MNC provides the initial stimulus to development; subsequently, emulation effects are transmitted to indigenous entrepreneurs, accelerating the progression of development. An example of the emulation effect is provided by S. Sethi and J. Sheth in the case of multinational investment in Glenrothis, Scotland:

> Once taboos against borrowing were broken, entrepreneurs obtained loans to start small supplier businesses, meeting the demands of multinational companies. . . . Soon some suppliers started to sell nationally throughout Britain. Others diversified into new products and developed whole new markets. Service groups and small production shops are forming to better serve these suppliers' needs.[59]

MNC subsidiaries vary greatly among themselves in structure and operation, depending upon product type, factor availability, regulatory environment, local competition, commercial strategy, and management style. As a result, the means by which MNCs are held responsible for affecting LDC entrepreneurship are similarly varied and numerous.

An evaluation of the MNC's impact upon LDC entrepreneurship is facilitated by prior enumeration of the various cited means of influence, both positive and negative. This task is undertaken within the framework of presenting the critical claims of dependency theorists— accompanied by the parallel presentation of the contradicting views of modernization theorists.

The critical claims of dependency theorists can be grouped into two general categories:

1. MNC preemption of potential entrepreneurs
   • employment effect
   • dissuasive effect
2. MNC displacement of existing entrepreneurs
   • displacement through purchase
   • displacement through competition

1. ENTREPRENEURIAL PREEMPTION

With respect to the first category, the preemption of indigenous entrepreneurship is claimed to occur along two separate dynamics— the "employment effect" and the "dissuasive effect."

Employment Effect

First, the "employment effect" is so termed because it refers to the MNC subsidiary's employment of indigenous managers who might otherwise engage in domestic entrepreneurial pursuits. Osvaldo Sunkel asserts that this activity is widespread among LDCs, with highly negative consequences: "The process of forming a local entrepreneurial class has been interrupted. The best talents that emerge from local industries are being absorbed into the new managerial class. . . . The elimination of the national entrepreneurial class necessarily excludes the possibility of self-sustained national development, along the lines of classical capitalist development."[60]

In this manner, Thomas Biersteker claims that the MNC subsidiary is aided in consolidating a position of competitive dominance within the LDC market: "By attracting their potential competitors with attractive wage scales, multinationals can add to the displacement of indigenous entrepreneurs, making them increasingly incapable of creating growth stimuli independently of international capitalism."[61]

The magnitude of this phenomenon is difficult to ascertain, because it is necessary to estimate the number of "would-be" entrepreneurs that might arise in the absence of MNC investment. However, a gross upper-limit estimation of the "employment effect" can be derived in recognizing that of the four million in the LDC workforce employed by MNCs in 1980,[62] no more than 6 percent were employed in the managerial ranks[63]—where most "would-be" entrepreneurs are assumed to be employed. As a hypothetical upper limit, this figure may seem relatively small; however, sheer quantity may be incidental when considering the impact that a relatively few exceptional people can have upon an economy. In a developing country, people with exceptional skills and talents have several indispensable roles that the Committee on the International Migration of Talent has designated crucial to development:

> 1) they constitute the intellectual bridge to the developed world; that is, they assess and adopt relevant ideas and technologies originating elsewhere; 2) they develop, maintain, and manage the production processes, the resources, and the complex structures of modern society; 3) as the intellectual elite, they bring about the structural and the institutional changes necessary if a nation is to become a modern state; and 4) their irreplaceable efforts, and the standards they set, heavily influence the educational and other institutions that shape future generations of educated persons.[64]

Dependency theorists charge that LDCs are being deprived of entrepreneurship, since the most capable indigenous talent is lost to MNC employment. This charge may be likened to "brain drain," a concept typically associated with the migration of students, physicians, engineers, or scientists from a lesser to a greater developed country. With respect to MNC subsidiaries, attaching the "brain drain" label is novel yet appropriate. Walter Adams's description of the classical brain drain process provides a conceptual structure for its elucidation: "Human capital, as a strategic resource, is flowing out of economies where it can make the greatest contribution to human welfare, and into economies already supplied with trained, capable, scientific and administrative personnel."[65] MNC subsidiaries may be viewed as funnels through which local brains are drained from an economy, transformed into profit through production and sale, and later repatriated abroad in the form of dividends. In this mode of brain drain, the local brains remain in the country, but only in the physical sense, for they are isolated within the corporate walls of the MNC and their productive capacity largely benefits extranational owners. This kind of brain drain is labeled "internal brain drain" (IBD) to distinguish it from the more familiar form.

In response, modernization theorists do not deny that MNCs employ talented indigenous labor endowed with entrepreneurial potential; however, they dispute the claim that the results are deleterious. Modernization theorists positively regard the MNC's effect upon LDC human capital because the MNC provides locally unavailable management training, skills, and experience to its indigenous managers. And, significantly, this talent is not viewed to be forever lost to the MNC subsidiary. Its employment by the MNC is not regarded as immutable, and it is expected that a significant number of MNC employees will venture into private entrepreneurship. Therefore the MNC subsidiary acts as a "breeder" firm, equipping managers with qualities crucial to entrepreneurial success. Mark Casson, in *The Entrepreneur,* suggests that there are four such crucial qualities: 1) imagination; 2) analytical ability; 3) foresight; and 4) computational skill.[66] All are innate to some extent; however, with the exception of imagination, each is susceptible to enhancement through training and work experience. In this respect, the MNC is considered exceptional, providing superior training and a rich and varied work experience to its employees. Consequently, in what Irving Gershenberg has labeled the "spread effect," indigenous MNC managers "then move on to disseminate their managerial knowhow by establishing their own firms, constituting the most significant contribution of multinational firms to the development of an indigenous cadre of managers."[67] Gershenberg warns, however, that transferred skills must be appropriate, otherwise, "the mobility of inappropriately trained managers will result in non-multinational firms emulating the worst features of foreign owned enterprise."[68] The effects of MNC training have been examined by the United Nation's International Labour Organization, which has concluded that "generally speaking . . . the subsidiaries of multinational corporations in developing host countries have had a beneficial effect on training."[69]

The dependencistas remain skeptical regarding the quality of MNC training, but in any case regard the spread effect to be minimal, as few MNC managers are expected to venture into self-employment, being content and secure in their MNC sinecures. Biersteker claims that superior wages and lacking external opportunities reinforce a disposition to remain with the MNC: "Multinationals can offer wage scales that make them more attractive than their indigenous competitors. They recruit the most talented labor, make independent ventures unattractive, and induce indigenous management personnel to manage a subsidiary rather than compete with it."[70]

Richard Caves has summarized evidence of the wage differential, asserting that an abundance of studies show that multinational enterprises (MNEs) pay higher wages than locally owned firms, citing studies by the U.S. Tariff Commission and by Grant L. Reuber regarding Mexico.[71] Furthermore, the pay differential appears to be most pronounced in LDCs with the least skilled workforces,[72] causing wages in these countries to be bid up in competition for the short supply of local skill and talent.

Nevertheless, MNEs cannot simply take their pick from local labor. Caves suggests that wage differentials between MNEs and national firms may collapse in cases where industry or size are controlled for.[73] Furthermore, even in countries with striking wage differentials between MNCs and local businesses, talented labor often has desirable alternatives to MNC employment. An example is provided in the case of a subsidiary of United Africa Company in Ghana, a distributor for Caterpillar equipment in that country. Here the firm recruited and employed students trained by the country's two top technical colleges. After two years of subsequent on-the-job training, many of the trainees departed in favor of more prestigious government jobs.[74]

MNCs do appear adept at luring talented indigenous labor; however, the ability of MNCs to retain those who would otherwise be inclined to venture out as entrepreneurs after a period of MNC employment is unclear and is a primary aspect of investigation in the present study.

To summarize the positions taken relative to the "employment effect" of entrepreneurial preemption, both modernization and dependency theorists agree that MNCs are generally successful in attracting talented indigenous labor in developing countries. Dependencistas argue that this practice inhibits development, for many of these persons would otherwise be entrepreneurs. Modernization theorists disagree, claiming that MNCs, with their superior technology and managerial practices, actually train entrepreneurs, equipping MNC managers with skills crucial to the success of the many who later establish their own businesses.

Dependencistas dispute the magnitude and significance of migration to entrepreneurship from the MNC. In instances where indigenous MNC managers become entrepreneurs, dependency theorists hesitate to recognize a lessening of dependence, because such new firms are claimed often to be tied to the former MNC employer in a dependent supplier relationship, where revenue from the "client" MNC determines the new firms' survival.

Dissuasive Effect

The "dissuasive effect" refers to the second type of MNC entrepreneurial preemption claimed by dependency theorists, whereby the MNC is perceived to dissuade indigenous entrepreneurship through market superiority and by depleting local financial credit and equity investment sources. For example, in Nigeria, Biersteker claims that "one of the major factors contributing to pre-emptive displacement . . . is the limited access of indigenous entrepreneurs to investment risk capital."[75] In the Nigerian case, a lack of sufficient LDC start-up capital was inferred from the fact that the majority of MNC financing of its LDC subsidiaries is raised in Nigeria.[76] As previously suggested in Chapter 2; however, it is likely that the problem is actually not a deficiency of capital, but rather a low demand for capital, due to a hesitance to initiate industrial enterprise. Entrepreneurial hesitance argues against a "capital shortage problem" but also brings up another potential dissuasive effect of the MNC subsidiary cited by E. O. Akeredolu-Ale:

> In a context where the local expatriate business community controlled most private entrepreneurial resources . . . and where the dominant "social world" of business was one to which the prospective indigenous entrepreneur did not belong and in which he could therefore not expect to operate effectively, many indigenous elements are likely to have been discouraged from making efforts by the mere fact that they did not perceive their chances of success to be good.[77]

Akeredolu-Ale claims that dissuasive preemption of entrepreneurs by MNCs has been profound in Nigeria: "the rise of a substantial indigenous owning class was precluded during the period which was most favorable for that event in the post-1946 period, and there was no sizable class of Nigerian entrepreneurs equipped, resource and experience wise, to venture into the modern forms of entrepreneurial activity which caught on in the period under review."[78]

In accord with Akeredolu-Ale's appraisal, Biersteker concludes that greater indigenous entrepreneurship would have been undertaken in Nigeria in the absence of MNC investment. In support, he cites Biafra's ability to develop indigenous production (fuel and weapons) when blockaded during its civil war with Nigeria, asserting that the "Biafran case suggests that feasible alternatives to the multinational corporation exists in Nigeria."[79] But Alan Rugman questions Biersteker's conclusion with respect to the Biafran case, seeing it as "more an example of a response to war conditions than a scientific experiment in alternative technology."[80] Biersteker supports his claim that indigenous enterprise would flourish and expand its scope in the absence of MNC competition by citing the success of indigenous firms in the textile, cement, and sawmilling industries, having in certain instances even displaced multinational firms.[81] However, Biersteker's evidence can support the opposite conclusion—that the success experienced by indigenous enterprise is attributable to the "spread effect" imparted by subsidiaries of foreign-based MNCs. Thus, MNC exodus might actually precipitate the stagnation of indigenous enterprise rather than stimulate an increase. Unfortunately, there is a lack of cases qualifying as suitable "experimental" tests of the MNC's dissuasive effect. For example, although Cuba, Tanzania, and China have attempted to develop without MNC investment, the fact that entrepreneurial cadres in these countries have not emerged to lead development does not constitute strong evidence in support of the MNC. In each country, increased hostility of the political environment to private domestic enterprise subsequent to insulation from fdi may just as well account for indigenous entrepreneurship's failure to replace the MNC and thrive in its absence.

2. ENTREPRENEURIAL DISPLACEMENT

Compared to entrepreneurial preemption, the displacement of existing entrepreneurs is a more visible phenomenon. The culpability of the MNC in this regard is alleged to arise through 1) its purchasing of indigenous enterprises and 2) its market superiority, which causes failure among indigenous competitors.

Displacement Through Purchase

With respect to the purchase of indigenous firms, a frequently cited study of the 187 largest U.S. firms in Latin America shows that between 1958 and 1967 U.S. firms established 1,309 subsidiaries. Those from whom information could be obtained revealed that more than 42 percent were initiated through the purchase of local enterprises.[82]

Nevertheless, in cases where MNCs have established their operations by purchasing local enterprise (e.g., Latin America), the net effect of the purchasing activity can only be evaluated properly by examining the uses to which the selling entrepreneurs apply their proceeds. For example, if an entrepreneur is bought out by an MNC and reinvests his proceeds by starting up a new enterprise, no net effect upon the absolute number of indigenously owned businesses would result. Additionally, the previous success experienced by the purchased indigenous firms must be examined to determine the qualitative significance of the displaced entrepreneur to the host economy.

Displacement Through Competition

In addition to the purchase of indigenous enterprises by MNCs, Biersteker claims that other local entrepreneurs are also displaced as a result of competition with MNC subsidiaries. "Many critics charge that [MNCs'] competitive advantage allows [them] to drive their indigenous competitors out of business. Multinational firms have international economic advantages because of their economies of scale, technology, management, selective access to new developments, trained personnel, markets, and financing."[83]

Modernization theorists discount the pervasiveness of this effect among LDCs. For example, Raymond Vernon acknowledges that MNC competition serves as a mechanism for local displacement but claims that "by and large, the area of concentration of the foreigners and that of local businessmen are quite distinct."[84] Therefore, dominance in a given industry by MNCs would likely result in only a small amount of local entrepreneurial displacement. In Biersteker's Nigerian study, MNC competition was not found to cause the dissolution of indigenous businesses. However, Vernon's reasons for this result were also not supported, for Nigerian and foreign-owned business did not concentrate in distinct industrial categories, but rather invested proportionately across industries.[85]

In general, of course, the modernization perspective looks favorably upon a vigorous multinational presence in the LDCs. Competitive displacement is not seen as being characteristically harmful to LDC development goals, although in cases where the MNC has little to offer in terms of capital, management, or technology, the net effect may indeed be adverse. Vernon claims this is especially the case "where foreign brand names are so overpowering as to wipe out local competitors who are capable of fabricating the same product."[86] While dependency theorists see the latter case as more the rule than the exception in the Third World, modernization theorists conclude the opposite. Upon MNC entry into an LDC market, the firms that go out of business first are typically considered the most wasteful, inefficient, and unprofitable. Others may arise to meet the foreign competition by raising their production standards, cutting costs, and investing in state-of-the-art machinery and equipment. As a result of the competition for market share and newly cultivated efficiency, domestic businesses may even end up pursuing export markets, opening up previously unavailable growth opportunities.

Aside from the competitive relationship between MNC subsidiaries and indigenous business enterprises, modernization theorists also emphasize the benefit to non-competing indigenous businesses from the role of the MNC subsidiary as a consumer of industrial goods. This is particularly true in more advanced LDCs, where subsidiaries of manufacturing MNCs are able to rely on locally produced raw materials and parts to fuel production. Expanding subsidiary sales cause the expansion of local suppliers and the founding of new businesses by indigenous entrepreneurs. Douglas Bennett and Kenneth Sharp have described the origin and success of the majority Mexican-owned automobile supplier industry, which has flourished by serving the interests of the transnationally owned domestic auto industry.[87] Indeed, linkages between MNC producers and domestic suppliers can be quite extensive. For example, a study of South Korean industry indicated that total employment (direct and indirect) by multinational enterprises was nearly two-thirds larger than that which they directly employed.

Dependencistas dispute the pervasiveness and benefit of MNC linkages to indigenous business, claiming that the MNCs generally find it more desirable to manufacture parts and raw materials in-house or to obtain them overseas. Furthermore, MNC linkages to indigenous suppliers are not viewed as promoting the goal of self-reliance. In the usual case, a situation of dependency is said to obtain, with the MNC representing a very large percentage of sales to the vulnerable indigenous supplier.

In summarizing the dependency and modernization theories' positions regarding the MNC's effect upon existing LDC entrepreneurs, both recognize the historical prevalence of buying out domestic enterprises when entering an LDC market; however, they strongly differ with respect to the overall effect of the MNC upon existing indigenous enterprises.

Dependency theorists view the effect as strongly negative. They claim that most businesses that are not purchased or priced out of the market by the MNC are left to eke out a marginal existence as an inherently inferior competitor. Viewed as more successful are those few local suppliers to the MNC subsidiary. Nevertheless, since these suppliers' operations are usually diverted toward exclusive production for MNC interests, their existence only contributes to a strengthening of foreign dependence.

Modernization theorists view these criticisms as misrepresenting the record of the MNC in the Third World. Overall, MNC activity is viewed as stimulating LDC entrepreneurship. While buyouts and shutdowns may result from MNC operations, such activity is generally considered to be progressive in its elimination of inefficient indigenous operators. Meanwhile, industrywide standards are lifted, output efficiency rises, markets expand, and new opportunities are availed to the prospective indigenous investor.

CHAPTER 4

Methodology

Through its impact upon indigenous entrepreneurship, the MNC subsidiary is claimed to influence the evolution of self-directed development in dependent countries. Dependencistas view the impact as overwhelmingly negative, with the multinational subsidiaries displacing existing entrepreneurs and inhibiting the emergence of new local enterprise. Modernization theorists criticize this interpretation and regard the MNC as a stimulus to indigenous entrepreneurship, diffusing technological and managerial know-how to local entrepreneurs and thereby enhancing their chances for commercial success.

In evaluating the validity of the competing theoretical perspectives, case study research was undertaken within the computer industries of Mexico and Canada. The choice of industry facilitates a comparison with prominent computer industry studies that have been previously discussed.[1]

The computer industry is an important sector for examination because underdeveloped countries consider it vital to their development plans.[2] According to the OECD, the computer industry belongs "to the main growth pole around which investment and production capacities will be structured as part of a new industrial revolution."[3] According to Peter Dicken, the computer industry, as a subset of the larger electronics industry, has

> extensive ramifications ... not only for other sectors of the economy but also for telecommunications and national defense ... [making] all governments increasingly anxious to avoid being left out or left behind in what is a rapidly moving technological scene. The electronics industry ... has come to be regarded as the touchstone of industrial success. Hence, all governments in the developed market economies, as well as those in the more industrialized developing countries operate substantial support programmes for the electronics industry, particularly microprocessors and computers.[4]

In Brazil and India, these programs consist of highly interventionist indigenization policies (see Chapter 3). Adler and Grieco hail such policies, concluding that the assertive bargaining strategies implemented by Brazil and India have achieved a marked lessening of dependency on foreign capital in their computer industries.

On the other hand, dependency has not been overcome in either country's computer industry, and the extent to which it has been reduced may have been overstated by Adler and Grieco. For instance, Peter Evans claims that, despite an increase of local capital accumulation in Brazil's computer industry, "the extent to which dependency has been 'reduced' is at least debatable [due to a] combination of reliance on foreign mainframes and their attendant operating systems software, dependence on imported silicon technology in all segments of the market, and the necessity of importing super-mini technology."[5]

Furthermore, the lack of efficiency currently demonstrated by Brazilian- and Indian-owned computer companies surely moderates the significance that can be attached to gains in local autonomy.

Modernization theory counsels against the heavy restrictions that have been imposed upon multinational computer firms in Brazil and India, favoring less intrusive institutional means for stimulating indigenous capacity. Dependencistas, however, deny any salutary effect of the MNC upon indigenous entrepreneurship and thus urge a complete break from multinational investment. Therefore, although for differing reasons, the modernization and dependency perspectives both criticize the form of state intervention practiced against MNCs in the Brazilian and Indian computer industries.[6]

The dependence and inefficiency of the Brazilian and Indian computer industries stimulate the search for desirable alternatives to state bargaining strategies. In choosing interventionist Brazil and India for study, Adler and Grieco seem to have discounted the utility of more liberal foreign investment regulations for reversing the degree of foreign dominance in highly dependent countries. The present study explores this alternative, evaluating the effects of the MNC upon indigenous entrepreneurship in the relatively more "MNC friendly" policy environments of Canada and Mexico. An overall positive MNC effect would lend support to the modernization perspective and argue against a state's pursuit of the slim "autonomy" benefits offered by a more hostile bargaining strategy. Conversely, a negative MNC effect upon indigenous entrepreneurship would support dependency theory and motivate recourse to more activist and radical state intervention against multinational investment.

Canada and Mexico, despite a wide discrepancy between their

development levels, were selected for investigation because of their high dependence upon the U.S. economy. Both governments are shown to be burdened by severe limitations on their ability to pursue national interests because they are constrained by divergent domestic special interests that detain economic progress and the parallel goal of reversing high levels of dependence. The political and economic data that follow describe the conditions more fully.

Political Data

Canada and Mexico gained independence from their European forbears in the 19th century. Canada, since its 1867 independence, and Mexico, subsequent to its 1910 revolution, have been characterized by relative stability in their political regimes—a goal eluding many other American countries.

Canada is a federal democracy whose constitution invests considerable authority in the provinces, resulting in a decentralization of political power that is unrivaled in other stable countries.[7] These constitutional arrangements have often checked the coherent exercise of federal power in Canada. Today, the challenges posed by Quebec separatism, the alienation of the Western provinces, and the continuing erosion of federal economic power to provincial control create significant difficulties for the federal system's attempt to advance the broader national interest. Nevertheless, the Canadian federal government is not without initiative, and it successfully promoted and negotiated a 1988 Free Trade Agreement with the United States and, despite great domestic opposition, is negotiating the North American Free Trade Agreement with the United States and Mexico.

Mexico is an authoritarian republic dominated since 1928 by the Institutional Revolutionary Party (PRI). Mexico's political leaders have far greater formal discretionary powers than their Canadian counterparts; however, in practice these powers do have significant constraints, limited in part by the revolutionary coalition from which their original mandate was derived. This coalition encompasses a disparate set of interests, including the agrarian, labor, and popular sectors of Mexican society. In addition, informal but disproportionately strong influence is exercised by industrial, commercial, and banking interests, further inhibiting the PRI's leadership.[8] As a result, Mexico's ruling elite generally find it necessary to restrain their exercise of power by adopting accomodationist policies which "minimize conflict between the various interests that are incorporated within the 'revolutionary family.'"[9] Surging inflation during the 1970s and 1980s exposed the ineffectiveness of the accomodationist approach. The government was unwilling to act decisively, hesitant to alienate either business or labor. As a result, wage and price controls were often short-lived. At other times, controls were supplemented by food subsidies that only enlarged the public debt burden, merely delaying the crisis. These accomodationist policies reveal the Mexican government's difficulty in acting in the nation's long term interests. Recently, however, President Carlos Salinas de Gortari has achieved success in reducing inflation by taking bold and unexpected political and economic reforms. Most notably, Salinas has accelerated the drive to reduce the scope of Mexico's public sector through privatization and has been an active promoter of free trade agreements with the United States and Canada, hoping these actions will lure greater inflows of foreign investment and lead Mexico to greater prosperity and development.

Thus, despite different formal powers, Canada and Mexico both portray a similar weakness in the exercise of federal power, inhibited by powerful special interests. Yet both federal governments are not without initiative or the ability to form national consensus.

Economic Data

Geographically contiguous to the United States, Canada and Mexico are financially dwarfed by their neighbor's $5 trillion economy, despite ranking eighth and twelfth, respectively, in Gross Domestic Product (GDP) worldwide.[10] The economic opportunities that this proximity affords Canada and Mexico are manifest in extensive bilateral commerce with the United States and large inflows of U.S. equity capital. Pursuant to these patterns, however, Canada and Mexico are especially vulnerable to changes in U.S. economic conditions and policies, often arousing nationalistic passions that seek a reversal of what are claimed to be trends of eroding sovereignty. Such sentiments are not surprising, for Canada and Mexico are generally acknowledged as being among the most dependent countries worldwide. Evidence of Canadian and Mexican dependency is observed in their concentration of import and export activity with the United States (see Table 1). For example, in 1985, 78 percent of Canadian exports and 58 percent of Mexican exports went to the United States.[11]

Trade dependence is compounded by high levels of U.S. direct

Table 1. Selected Economic and Demographic Data of Mexico, Canada, and the United States (1988)

		Mexico	Canada	U.S.
1.	National Income Per Capita (1985, $U.S.)	$1,990	$11,778	$14,565
	Gross Domestic Product Data			
2.	GDP ($U.S. billions) (1985)	$177.5	$348.9	$3,947.0
3.	GDP Real Growth Rate (1980-1985)	1.6%	2.5%	2.4%
	Population Data			
4.	Population (millions) (1985)	78.5	25.4	239.2
5.	Real Growth Rate of Population (1980-1985)	2.5%	1.1%	1.0%
	Export Data (1985)			
6.	Exports ($U.S. billions)	$22.2	$90.8	$213.1
7.	Exports (% of GDP)	12.5%	26.0%	5.4%
8.	% of Total Exports to U.S.	58.0%	78.0%	—
	Import Data (1985)			
9.	Imports ($U.S. billions)	$14.0	$81.1	$361.6
10.	Imports (% of GDP)	7.9%	23.2%	9.2%
11.	$ of Total Imports From U.S.	66.0%	71.0%	—
	Technology Indicators			
12.	Years Schooling (1980) (percentile among all countries)	63.0%	97.0%	100.0%
13.	Share of Academic Labor in Total Workforce (1980) (percentile among all countries)	41.0%	84.0%	84.0%
14.	Share of Nobel Prize Winners (1970-1979) (percentile among all countries)	45.0%	90.0%	100.0%

1.–11., *The World in Figures* (London: Economist Publications, 1988)
12.–14., G. P. Muller, *Comparative World Data* (Baltimore: Johns Hopkins University Press, 1988).

investment in the Canadian and Mexican economies. In fact, the United States is far and away the largest investor in its bordering neighbors, accounting for large production shares of many Mexican and Canadian industries. For instance, as of 1981, the share of production by foreign firms in the manufacturing industry of Mexico was 39 percent.[12] In the Mexican computer industry, the infiltration is even more pronounced, with subsidiaries of U.S. firms presently accounting for nearly 100 percent of domestic production of finished computers.[13] In Canada, data from 1981 reveal foreign firms having a 56.6 percent production share in domestic manufacturing,[14] making it easy to see why Canada has been described as the largest branch plant economy in the world. Indeed, Europeans often apply the term Canadianization when referring to the threat of higher levels of industrial dependency in their own countries.[15] As in Mexico, foreign dominance in the Canadian computer industry is particularly pronounced, with foreign firms (largely of U.S. origin) accounting for approximately 95 percent of finished computer sales.[16]

Although Mexico has a lower level of trade dependence and foreign investment concentration in its domestic economy, its position of dependence upon the United States is compounded by its continuing, although recently decreasing, difficulty in servicing more than $80 billion in external debt, the majority owed to U.S. creditors. The debtor/creditor relationship confers an additional source of U.S. leverage over the Mexican economy, making additional credits and possible debt forgiveness contingent upon adherence to U.S.-prescribed changes in Mexican policy. Mexican dependence is further amplified by its weak economy. A per capita national income of $1,990 in 1985 justifies its classification as an LDC, notwithstanding its classification as a Newly Industrialized Country (see Table 1).[17] Mexico desperately needs to accelerate and diversify its industrialization in order to support a population in which more than a quarter are still engaged in agriculture, despite this sector generating only nine percent of GDP (see Table 2). The crisis is especially acute for Mexico, straining to stay even under mounting pressures to feed a burgeoning population that grew at an average rate of 2.5 percent during the 1980–1985 period (during this same period, Mexican GDP averaged only 1.6 percent [see Table 1]).[18] To achieve necessary growth, Mexico seeks to displace its intensive reliance upon oil (see Table 3),[19] whose collapsing prices, beginning in 1981, were foremost in initiating the deep recession that extended through most of the decade.

Table 2. Structure of Mexican and Canadian Gross Domestic Product and
Labor Force (1984)

By Origin	% of GDP		% of Labor Force	
	Mexico	Canada	Mexico	Canada
Agriculture	9%	3%	26%	5%
Mining and Quarrying	10	6	2	2
Manufacturing	24	17	12	17
Elec., Gas, and Water	1	4	1	1
Construction	5	4	6	6
Distribution and Hotels	23	9	8	17
Transport and Communications	7	7	3	6
Other	22	50	43	45
Total	100%	100%	100%	100%

The World in Figures (London: Economist Publications, 1988).

Canada, of course, is far wealthier than Mexico, with a GDP more than twice as large. Furthermore, its wealth is produced by a population of less than a third of Mexico's, and Canadian living standards, in terms of per capita income, are among the highest worldwide (see Table 1).[20] Also, Canada is far more diversified than Mexico in its export base, and is thus less vulnerable, with automotive production the leading source of export revenue, accounting for 27 percent of its total exports (see Table 4).[21] In addition, Canada is among the more technologically advanced economies, aided by its U.S.-supported industrial base and reinforced by advanced indigenous scientific capabilities, indicated from high levels of student enrollment, academic labor, and Nobel Prize Winners (see Table 1).[22] Also, Canada is characterized by relatively low income inequality,[23] and strong social programs give extensive support to the disadvantaged. Nevertheless, dependencistas hold foreign MNCs responsible for other ills in Canada, most notably for its lack of indigenous industrial entrepreneurship and for a comparative advantage in trade which is reflected in the export of raw and partially processed materials,[24] a pattern typically associated with less developed countries. For example, more than 27 percent of Canada's export trade is in raw materials, composed of energy products (9.4 percent), forestry products (14.6 percent), and metal ores (3.4 percent). Dependencistas view this pattern of trade as disadvantageous, citing a long term secular decline in the terms of trade (i.e., export prices relative to

Table 3. Mexican Import and Export Data (1988)

Main Imports (1984)	% of total	Main Import Sources	
Machinery	23%	United States	66%
Chemicals	14	Japan	4
Food	12	West Germany	4
(of which, cereals 7)		France	2
Iron and steel	6	Brazil	2
Motor vehicles	5		
Ships	4		
Soybeans	4		
Instruments	3		

Main Exports (1984)	% of total	Main Export Destination	
Crude oil	62%	United States	58%
Machinery	5	Japan	8
Petroleum products	5	Spain	7
Chemicals	4	United Kingdom	4
Fruit and Vegetables	3	France	4
Non-ferrous ores	2		
Motor vehicles	2		
Shrimps	2		
Coffee	2		

The World in Figures (London: Economist Publications, 1988).

import prices) for raw material and other primary product export-ers.[25]

Given their perspective on Canada's relationship with the U.S., dependencistas claim that the realization of the important national goals of greater economic self reliance and self direction is precluded. Thus, Canada is well suited for an examination of the MNC's effects upon indigenous entrepreneurship, for the expansion of this activity is considered requisite for a country's attainment of self-reliant and self-directed development.

Indigenous entrepreneurship in the Mexican computer industry is also examined. As a relatively advanced LDC, Mexico compares in stature to Brazil and India. Grieco has commented that Mexico possesses an industrial potential to benefit from a state-guided indi-genization drive similar to India's: "India's industrial structure is simi-lar to Brazil's and Mexico's. . . . Brazil and Mexico match or exceed

Table 4. Canadian Import and Export Data (1988)

Main Imports (1985)	% of total	Main Import Sources	
Motor Vehicles	28%	United States	71%
(of which parts 14,		Japan	6
passenger cars 11)		United Kingdom	3
Machinery, non-electric	14	West Germany	3
Electrical machinery	11		
Chemicals	6		
Food	5		
Crude oil	4		
Instruments	3		
Metal small	2		
manufacturers			

Main Imports from
United States

Motor vehicles	34
(of which parts 19,	
passenger cars 12)	
Machinery, non-electric	15
Electrical machinery	12
Chemicals	6

Main Exports (1985)	% of total	Main Export Destination	
Motor vehicles	27%	United States	78%
(of which passenger		Japan	5
cars 14, parts 8, lorries 5)		United Kingdom	2
Machinery	11	Soviet Union	1
Crude oil and products	7		
Chemicals	5		
Newsprint	5		
Timber	4		
Natural Gas	4		
Non-ferrous metals	4		

Table 4. Continued

Main Exports (1985)	% of total
Main Exports to United States	
Motor vehicles	34%
(of which passenger cars 17, parts 9, lorries 7)	
Machinery	11
Crude oil and products	9
Natural gas	5
Newsprint	5
Chemical	4
Timber	4

The World in Figures (London: Economist Publications, 1988).

India in terms of financial resources available per science and technology worker. Hence, India's bargaining success with multinationals might also be achieved by Brazil and Mexico at present."[26]

But in light of the skepticism elsewhere expressed with respect to the claimed benefits of a vigorous bargaining strategy, a more thorough exploration of the MNC's effects upon Mexican entrepreneurship in the current policy environment is warranted.

In evaluating the Mexican and Canadian computer industries, the activities of the wholly owned, resident subsidiaries of Control Data Corporation (CDC) were examined. CDC is a U.S.-owned multinational corporation founded in 1957 and headquartered in Bloomington, Minnesota. CDC is a major competitor in the international computer industry, generating revenues of $1.7 billion in 1990 (28 percent of that total was derived from international operations).[27] The company specializes in large-scale computers and peripheral equipment and provides extensive data processing services.

CDC-Mexico has its headquarters and major operations in Mexico City. The company has a different product mix than its U.S. parent, due to the less developed Mexican computer market and technological requirements. Whereas CDC-U.S. perceives itself as primarily oriented toward the scientific, technical, and engineering market for the manipulation of complex databases with mainframes, the Mexican subsidiary is oriented to serving high-volume data processing needs. For these purposes, minicomputers (and a much smaller number of mainframes) manufactured in the United States are sold or leased to Mexican clients through the subsidiary. In addition, a significant fraction of revenues is derived from systems consulting, servicing and repairs, and software development and sales.

CDC-Canada is headquartered in Toronto, Ontario, the location of its commercial products division. The Toronto division accounts for approximately 50 percent of CDC-Canada's revenues. The complement of subsidiary revenues derives from the government systems division—Computing Devices—situated in Ottawa, Ontario. Computing Devices is autonomous from Toronto management, operating as a virtually distinct subsidiary and reporting directly to U.S. headquarters. Computing Devices activities include the design and production of advanced electronic equipment such as tactical navigation systems for airplanes, fire control computers for tanks, and acoustic signal processors for the detection of submarines. Computing Devices also distributes Control Data hardware and accessory equipment. In the present study, Computing Devices was isolated for examination in order to focus the scope of inquiry.

Highlighting the international operations of a single MNC creates difficulties for generalizing results to the industry as a whole. Nevertheless, it is argued that the sacrifice in breadth was justified by the depth and coverage provided by the chosen methodology. Personal, in-depth interviews with entrepreneurs were permitted by the focused approach, enabling an enriched and extensive evaluation of the mechanisms of MNC stimulated entrepreneurship.[28] Furthermore, in assessing the entrepreneurial "spread effect" due to multinational employment, restricting the methodological purview to CDC enabled almost complete coverage of the entire set of CDC's entrepreneurial ex-employees.[29] This achievement is significant, because it avoids the multitude of biases that might have arisen with sampling, a technique that would have been necessitated by an industrywide study. Furthermore, time and financial limitations would have made it exceedingly difficult to obtain sufficient sample coverage in an industrywide study.

Of course, mailed questionnaires, despite their lack of depth, would have circumvented the financial and time limitations associated with personal interviews. However, previous entrepreneurial research has revealed that questionnaire return rates are quite low (ranging from 15 to 25 percent for Canadian businesses).[30] In addition, survey questionnaire respondents often differ in attitude from non-respondents, making it difficult to extrapolate results.

Yet tradeoffs are unavoidable, and the issue of generalizing results remains. In concession to this problem, the evaluation of results will include discussion of corporate features that seem distinctive to CDC among its multinational peers. Host governments might urge multinationals to adopt entrepreneurially enhancing features that appear to be unique to CDC, and likewise discourage CDC's entrepreneurially inhibiting features.

The evaluation of CDC's effects upon indigenous entrepreneurship was facilitated by Canadian and Mexican contacts obtained through executive personnel of CDC-U.S. Canadian and Mexican executives were contacted by telephone and later personally interviewed. Telephone contact was intended to obtain information relative to past employees who later became entrepreneurs; personal interviews sought information relating to company history, current operations, acquisition activity, and government influences upon CDC operations. Where relevant, executive testimony was corroborated and supplemented by publicly available materials and interviews with ex-employees of CDC.

Interviewed ex-employees were those who had initiated a business venture subsequent to departure from CDC. These entrepreneurs were located with the assistance of current CDC personnel and through other entrepreneurs. In both Canada and Mexico, multiple references assured the identification of all significant entrepreneurs with previous CDC employment. The entrepreneurs were personally interviewed,[31] and information relating to their employment history, entrepreneurial records, and personal characteristics was elicited. In addition, interviewees' assessments of factors influencing their own entrepreneurship were obtained.

The information compiled from the combined data sources was utilized to assess the validity of the claims of the dependency writers regarding the MNC's effects upon indigenous entrepreneurship (see Chapter 3). Next, the methodology utilized to evaluate the various cited effects is described.

Entrepreneurial Preemption

1. EMPLOYMENT EFFECT

Of the subcategories which comprise the alleged MNC effects upon indigenous entrepreneurship, the employment effect is manifested most directly, for as an employer, the MNC subsidiary conditions the character of indigenous human capital firsthand.

In assessing the employment effect, direct empirical measurement of the entrepreneurship prevented by MNC employment (i.e., internal brain drain) relative to the amount activated (i.e., the spread effect) would be ideal. Regrettably, IBD can not be directly observed but must be inferred more holistically, through a "creative" interpretation of available data in the effort to validate conterfactual assertions (e.g., if not for the MNC, indigenous entrepreneurship would decrease). Observing the MNC spread effect is also problematic. While it is possible to observe the enterprises initiated by former MNC employees directly, it is difficult to determine whether MNC employment facilitated this "spreading" or merely served to postpone entrepreneurship that would have been initiated earlier. Problems of this type are endemic to macropolitical studies, where the investigator is unable to manipulate the independent variables (in this case, the MNC and the policy environment) in order to isolate their effects. Fortunately, this limitation does not prevent a critical evaluation of development theories. In the social sciences, the results of empirical testing are often ambiguous, unable to "distinguish between 'correct' and 'incorrect' theories or explanations."[32] Yet dominant theoretical paradigms often do emerge, swaying the intellectual community through non-empirical, holistic arguments which appeal to the theory's sense of coherence with general social, political, and economic knowledge. Of course, this activity is generally more lenient than empirical approaches in allowing ideological biases to permeate the research process. Thus, in the current study, "second best" holistic methodologies are employed only where empirical measurement is deemed unfeasible.

Internal Brain Drain and the MNC spread effect represent entrepreneurial flows in the opposite direction—to, and from, the MNC. Previous studies have not attempted to quantify the magnitude of these flows, although modernization and dependency theorists have been uninhibited in respectively exhorting the benefits and disadvantages of MNC investment to indigenous entrepreneurship. For the most part, quantitative, systematic, and direct evidence of indigenous entrepreneurs in their relationship to the MNC are not provided. Attempting to avoid this oversight, a contribution of the current study is to provide quantitative measurement in estimating the spread effect from CDC's Mexican and Canadian subsidiaries. This measurement is assessed with respect to national autonomy goals and weighed against non-empirical evidence of IBD to present an overall assessment of CDC's effect in preempting indigenous entrepreneurship through employment.

A. Spread Effect

To assess the spread effect, interviews were conducted with former employees of CDC-Mexico and Computing Devices (Canada) who became entrepreneurs after their MNC tenure. A gross measure of the spread effect was derived through comparing the sum of current business revenue of the subject entrepreneurs with the revenue of their associated MNC subsidiary.

In addition, the subsidiaries' role in facilitating observed entrepreneurship was evaluated. This was accomplished by correlating objective measures of the CDC employment experience (years employed and level in corporate hierarchy) for each entrepreneur with the degree of his subsequent entrepreneurial success (measured by business revenue). Those MNC variables that were found to be strongly associated with entrepreneurial success were then evaluated for their possible role in stimulating successful entrepreneurship. The independent assessment of causation by the subject entrepreneurs was the source of evidence.

Lastly, the significance of the observed entrepreneurship to a lessening of dependency was interpreted from certain characteristics of the entrepreneurs' businesses. Among the features examined were export sales, product type, and percent of sales to the MNC subsidiary. A high level of exports, a high level of product sales in direct competition with the MNC subsidiary, and a low fraction of total revenue earned from sales to the subsidiary were each considered supportive of the goal of lessened foreign dependence.

B. Internal Brain Drain

In assessing the opposing entrepreneurial flow, IBD, it is necessary to determine the probable activities that the subjects would have engaged in if not for their employment with CDC. As a measure of this, interview subjects who reported having had job interviews with indigenously owned and controlled organizations just prior to employment by CDC are regarded as possessing no serious interest in entrepreneurship, depreciating the IBD charge. Otherwise, evidence that entrepreneurship was a strongly considered vocational alternative at the time of CDC employment is considered indicative of IBD, suggesting that the employment opportunity presented by CDC caused people to forego entrepreneurship.

Of course, aside from its initial employment of would-be entrepreneurs, it is charged that the MNC subsidiary is able to retain this talent by offering superior financial incentives. Relative to this claim, CDC salaries were evaluated with respect to their disparity from those offered by government and by indigenously owned firms in the computer/electronics industry. High disparities in CDC's favor would suggest a superior ability to retain indigenous talent once employed, discouraging entrepreneurial initiative through raising the opportunity cost associated with foregone employment.

2. DISSUASIVE EFFECT

A. Market Superiority

The effort to determine the degree to which MNC market superiority dissuades indigenous entrepreneurial initiative is plagued by the previously discussed methodological limitation, that is, of having to estimate the level of indigenous entrepreneurship that would have arisen in the absence of multinational investment. This difficulty was illustrated in Chapter 3, in the discussion of Biersteker's study of the effects of MNC investment upon indigenous entrepreneurship in Nigeria. Unfortunately, better methodologies are unavailable; therefore, the current study relies upon holistic assessments in ascertaining the magnitude of latent entrepreneurship that is intimidated and inhibited by CDC's Canadian and Mexican subsidiaries. Insights developed from research interviews are considered in light of general knowledge of the Canadian and Mexican computer industries in ascertaining CDC's dissuasive effect upon indigenous entrepreneurship.

B. Capital Availability

The composition of debt and equity capital represented in the CDC subsidiaries' initial funding and current financing is evaluated, determining the amount derived from indigenous sources in order to gauge possible diversion from indigenous entrepreneurship.

Entrepreneurial Displacement

1. DISPLACEMENT THROUGH PURCHASE

CDC-Mexico's and Computing Devices' activities in buying out indigenous businesses as part of their initial investment or in their efforts to expand were determined through interviews with corporate personnel and corroborated by former employee interviewees and publicly available materials.

The absence of CDC activity in this regard negated the necessity for significant evaluation of the qualitative aspects of this displacement mode.

2. DISPLACEMENT THROUGH COMPETITION

The effect of CDC Mexico and Computing Devices in driving indigenous entrepreneurs out of business is assessed. It is recognized that this effect is mediated by the possible enhancement of efficiency stimulated in surviving indigenous firms.

Strong evidence of competitive displacement in Mexico and Canada was expected to be slight in the finished computer market as this domain has always been a bastion of almost complete dominance by foreign MNCs; however, the prevalence of competitive displacement in associated products was surmised from the interview data of competing entrepreneurs.

CHAPTER 5

Results

Entrepreneurial Preemption

1. EMPLOYMENT EFFECTS

A. The Spread Effect

Canadian and Mexican entrepreneurs formerly employed by Control Data subsidiaries were interviewed in order to examine the effect of this employment experience upon their entrepreneurship.

In Canada, 16 entrepreneurs associated with 14 enterprises were identified.[1] Entrepreneurs from 12 of these firms were personally interviewed.[2] The 14 firms were established between 1962 and 1981, and all but one remained in business or had been sold to a larger company at the time data was collected in late 1988.[3] The businesses range from $400,000 to $125 million in annual revenue and produce a broad variety of proprietary computer products sold worldwide to governments and private industry (see Table 5).[4] Most of the businesses undertake significant research and development activities while several also engage in consulting.

Although Computing Devices sells 90 to 95 percent of its production to the defense industry, its alumni entrepreneurs have branched out, receiving about 63 percent of their combined revenue from other commercial areas (see Table 5). They have achieved high levels of efficiency in their operations, demonstrated by rapid growth and export success (70 percent of combined entrepreneur revenue is from export sales [see Table 5]). In Canada, the businesses started by the entrepreneurs generated combined revenue of approximately $232 million during calendar year 1987,[5] well surpassing Computing Devices' $100 million for the same period.

In Mexico, 14 entrepreneurs were identified and nine personal interviews were conducted. Of the 14 entrepreneurs, 11 own CDC service franchises, providing each with a 25 percent share of revenue earned from computer services and repairs performed for CDC computer owners and lessees.[6] Often the franchisees also distribute CDC

Table 5. Entrepreneurs' Business Data (I)

Canada

Entre ID #	Entrepreneurs' Business Activity	(D) Entre Revenue (000's)	(D') **** Rank ****	% Export (of rev.)	% Defense (of rev.)
C1	Software Development	$3,200	6	0%	80%
C2	Satellite Imagery	2,538	5	78	0
C3*	Former Partner of C2	0	1	—	—
C4	Electronic Security	8,000	9	80	0
C5	Combustion Analysis	400	2.5	10	0
C6	Factory Info. Systems	4,000	7.5	90	0
C7	Factory Info. Systems	400	2.5	0	0
C8	Display Technology	20,000	12	80	100
C9	Airborn Systems	4,000	7.5	0	25
C10*	Airborn Systems	12,159	11	—	—
C11	R & D Signal Proc.	600	4	10	50
C12	Crash Indicators	28,514	13.5	80	100
C13*	Former Partner of C12	28,514	13.5	80	100
C14	Graphics & Consulting	8,800	10	43	50
C15	Laser Imaging	49,554	15	87	0
C16	Systems Networking	64,000	16	70	0
	Total**	$232,140		$163,417	$85,287
				(export $)	(defense $)

* did not interview (business folded year after C2's departure)
** totals not including C2 data

Mexico

Entre ID #	Entrepreneurs' Business Activity	(D) Entre Revenue	(D') **** Rank ****	% Export (of rev.)	% Defense (of rev.)
M1+	Training	$ 21,200	5	0%	0%
M2+	Comp. Supplies Sales	5,333	1.5	0	0
M3	Potato Farm	124,200	7	0	0
M4+	Partner of M3	7,200	3	0	0
M5+	Computer Sales	5,333	1.5	0	0
M6	Comp. Serv. & Repairs	52,980	6	0	0

Table 5. Continued

Entre ID #	Entrepreneurs' Business Activity	(D) Entre Revenue	(D') **** Rank ****	% Export (of rev.)	% Defense (of rev.)
M7 +	Franchise Only	11,920	4	0	0
M8	Computer Distr., Software Dev., etc...	5,849,889	9	new contract	0
M9	Partner of M8	2,924,945	8	new contract	0
	Total	$9,003,000			

+ CDC franchisee

computer products. Otherwise, they freely pursue business opportunities not associated with CDC.[7] The interviewed former employees of CDC-Mexico generated combined revenues of approximately $9 million from their businesses in 1988 (see Table 5). Although not as impressive as the performance by Canadian entrepreneurs, this figure is nevertheless substantial, comparing in order of magnitude to CDC-Mexico's revenue of $30 million for the same period. Of the $9 million, the bulk is attributable to the operations of two entrepreneurs,[8] both former CDC-Mexico employees who together own a computer distributorship, established in 1982. With 80 percent of their revenue coming from sales of Hewlett-Packard computers, their business grossed nearly $6 million in 1988,[9] and they employed 50 people in their Mexico City headquarters and 25 to 30 sales associates nationwide.[10] Despite their tremendous success, both predict a tenuous future for Mexican computer distributors. With the gradual opening of the Mexican borders to U.S. imports, significant market share has been lost to U.S.-based distributors. Furthermore, competition from secondhand computer clearing houses is a growing problem, causing them to worry that many among their ranks will be forced to shut down. Consequently, they have placed greater emphasis on a small but growing aspect of their business—software. With their CDC technical training, varied management backgrounds, and strong educations,[11] they have been able to develop, install, and service a variety of software products. They claim that the customized nature of business software allows them to avoid the highly competitive sales environment associated with their major product line. A recent major success in their software operations was a large sale (and an accompanying analysis contract) to PepsiCo, Inc., in Guatemala.

The remaining enterprises formed by former CDC-Mexico employees have all been initiated since 1984. Despite their relatively modest revenue, these businesses are quite promising, and they have weathered serious national crises (e.g., hyperinflation, an earthquake, and dropping oil prices) while typically remunerating their owners several times more than that which they obtained during their CDC employment (during the same period average real wages in Mexico declined).[12]

Five of these smaller enterprises are franchises (see Table 5). The franchise idea was conceived and promoted by CDC-Mexico in consultation with U.S. corporate headquarters as a means to lower subsidiary overhead and stimulate productivity by conferring the financial and psychological advantages of ownership to service engineers.[13]

Economic conditions in Mexico prompted CDC's decision to set up franchises. In recent years, Mexico's attempts to emerge from its debt crisis and attract foreign capital have been accompanied by fiscal austerity measures, resulting in decreased government services and purchases (sales to state-owned enterprises generally account for 80 percent of CDC-Mexico's annual revenue). At the same time, computers have become cheaper and more reliable, reducing both sales and service revenue per unit.

Mindful of these trends, CDC-Mexico determined in 1984 that service revenue would soon be unable to support the salary and overhead of service engineers in certain market locations. The franchise scheme provided an alternative, and increased productivity in the delivery of computer services was achieved by providing the entrepreneur with financial incentives. Employees were strongly encouraged toward franchise status; however, CDC recognized that educated and trained engineers are not easily replaced in Mexico, affording its employees the freedom to reject the franchise offer. In fact, CDC-Mexico executives express disappointment for not being able to persuade more service engineers to become franchisees.[14] The typical service engineer was described as risk-averse and thus reluctant to accept the increased managerial responsibilities of self-employment, despite the greater financial reward expected from a relatively secure flow of service contract revenue.[15]

Reservations notwithstanding, 11 former CDC-Mexico employees now own and operate service franchises. Since 1984, these franchises have succeeded in significantly cutting subsidiary costs and supporting Mexican entrepreneurship. Of the six franchise entrepreneurs interviewed, two had started their businesses within just six months of being interviewed, and CDC contract revenue still represented virtually 100 percent of their incomes. Yet in both cases, plans had already been made and steps taken to solicit income from non-CDC clients.[16] Both entrepreneurs cited their CDC base revenue as essential in providing financial security to support their ventures into riskier but potentially more lucrative endeavors.

The four remaining franchise entrepreneurs commenced business in 1984. Only one of the four has not sought revenue opportunities outside of CDC.[17] The other three entrepreneurs have managed to bring in additional employees and have considerably expanded their base of service revenue beyond CDC contracts, providing services for competing computer systems. In addition, franchisees have expanded the range of their activities.[18] Together, all have taken significant risks and have shown considerable initiative in expanding their businesses and laying plans for future growth. As these businesses expand beyond their CDC base revenue, the entrepreneurs gain in autonomy and self-direction, having utilized an initially dependent status as a springboard to increased commercial independence and financial success.

The amount of revenue earned by former CDC employees in Canada and Mexico suggests possible subsidiary responsibility for the output through its conferral of valuable technical, financial, and managerial experiences to its employees, among whom many later venture out as entrepreneurs. Of course, further evidence for this possibility is needed, since employment in itself does not constitute strong evidence of a critical role for CDC in the success of the entrepreneurs. For many, CDC employment was only one of a series of jobs preceding entrepreneurship. A few of the many other factors that may have contributed to their entrepreneurial initiative and success include a strong education, personal wealth, and an assertive personality. Thus, the CDC employment experience is more thoroughly scrutinized in order to assess its potential prominence among the entire configuration of influences contributing to entrepreneurial success.

The decisions and actions of a founding entrepreneur are perhaps the single most critical determinant of an enterprise's success. Thus, it is sensible to assume that the quality of skills and business experiences an entrepreneur possesses at the initiation of a business will have a profound impact on the likelihood of its future success. Arnold C. Cooper, in the *Encyclopedia of Entrepreneurship,* confirms this expectation through a survey of the literature, concluding that

> despite some mixed findings, success generally attended those entre-
> preneurs who were better educated, who had relevant managerial and
> industrial experience, who had owned previous businesses, who started
> businesses similar to those they had left, who were involved in a found-
> ing team, who had more initial capital, and who had systematically
> sought the advice of professional advisors as they started their firms.[19]

From among the aforementioned factors, those directly associated with CDC employment are managerial and industrial experience.[20] Precise measurement of the degree of managerial and industrial experience obtained by entrepreneurs during their CDC employment is, of course, impossible; nevertheless, the number of years
employed by CDC might be a rough indicator of the relative magnitude of industrial experience received during this period.

Canadian and Mexican entrepreneurs were found to have been
previously employed by CDC for an average of seven and nine years,
respectively (see Table 6). This period was significant for most entrepreneurs, representing a substantial portion of their average years of
pre-entrepreneurial experience in the computer/electronics industry—67 percent in Canada and 81 percent in Mexico.

However, statistical analysis did not confirm an association between the number of years employed by CDC and subsequent entrepreneurial success (defined as gross revenue in the entrepreneurs'
most recent fiscal year, adjusted to 1988 dollars) in either Canada or
Mexico (see Table 7). Thus, while entrepreneurs may have received
certain experiential benefit through their period of CDC employment, the amount of time employed by CDC does not in itself help
distinguish the prospects for future entrepreneurial success.

A more sensitive measure of the influence of the CDC work
experience would incorporate qualitative dimensions, highlighting
the most significant. In this context, it is recognized that the richness,
challenge, and variety of an employment experience increases with
movement up the corporate ladder. Indeed, for a prospective entrepreneur, prior exposure to such executive functions as budgeting and
long-term planning represents a valuable background experience.
Thus, the level of responsibility attained in the CDC corporate hier-

Table 6. Work Experience Prior to Entrepreneurship

Canada

Entre ID#	(A) Highest Responsibility of Entrepreneur with Control Data Corp	(A') **** Rank ****	(B) Years CDC Exper.	(B') **** Rank ****	(C) Years Total Exper.	(B/C) % CDC Years
C1	Software Group Leader	1.5	5	4	10	50%
C2	Division Manager	12.5	14	13	22	64
C3*	Project Engineer	4.5	—	—	—	—
C4	Division Manager	12.5	9	11.5	9	100
C5	Project Manager	7.5	7	7.5	10	70
C6	Division Director	12.5	8	9.5	10.5	76
C7	Software Group Leader	1.5	5	4	8	63
C8	Project Engineer	4.5	5	4	10	50
C9	Asst. Chief Engineer	9	5	4	20.5	24
C10*	Chief Engineer	12.5	—	—	—	—
C11	Project Engineer	4.5	9	11.5	10.5	86
C12	Division Director	12.5	5	4	5	100
C13*	Division Director	12.5	—	—	—	—
C14	Project Manager	7.5	8	9.5	13	62
C15	Asst. General Manager	16	7	7.5	8.5	82
C16	Project Engineer	4.5	4	1	9	44
	Mean =		7		11.2	67

* did not interview

archy can be hypothesized to vary positively with subsequent entrepreneurial success. Hierarchical position cannot be quantitatively measured; therefore, entrepreneurs were ranked. Fortuitously, there was wide range among entrepreneurs on the responsibility dimension in both countries, giving the measure a broad context. In Canada, the entrepreneurs' previous jobs ranged from the former second in command at Computing Devices to a low-level supervisor. In Mexico, a former CDC-Mexico president and an entry-level service engineer spanned the range of prior responsibility levels.

Table 6. Continued

Mexico

Entre ID#	(A) Highest Responsibility of Entrepreneur with Control Data Corp	(A') **** Rank ****	(B) Years CDC Exper.	(B') **** Rank ****	(C) Years Total Exper.	(B/C) % CDC Years
M1+	Group Leader	5	8	5.5	8	100%
M2+	Chief Repair Engineer	4	10	7	10	100
M3	Operations Manager	7.5	19	9	19	100
M4+	Customer Engineer	1.5	4	1	4	100
M5+	Customer Engineer	1.5	7	3.5	7	100
M6	Super., Cust. Engineer	6	7	3.5	8	88
M7+	Customer Engineer	3	12	8	16	75
M8	Sales Manager	7.5	8	5.5	20	40
M9	General Manager	9	6	2	23	26
	Mean =		9.0		12.8	81%

+ franchisee

Statistical analysis provides strong support for the responsibility hypothesis, revealing a significant association between CDC managerial level (i.e., industry experience) and business revenue (i.e., entrepreneurial success) for entrepreneurs in both Canada and Mexico (see Table 7). These results support the view that the managerial and industrial experiences obtained with CDC are instrumental in equipping future entrepreneurs with the tools for business success; however, this inference is tentative. In fact, what is actually "proven" is that high ranking CDC managers tend to be more successful entrepreneurs than lower ranking managers.[21] It may be the case that previous work experiences, personality traits, and academic capabilities fostered upward mobility in the CDC corporate ladder, and that these same traits and capabilities also engendered subsequent entrepreneurial success. Such an emphasis tends to diminish the likelihood of an MNC "spread effect." Upon further investigation, however, additional support for a CDC spread effect was revealed.

Table 7. Statistical Correlations

	Canada	Mexico
1. Years CDC Experience	(B) X (D)	(B') X (D')
by Entrepreneur Revenue	r = -0.38 +	r = 0.046*
	(p > .10)	(p > .10)
2. Management Responsibility CDC	(A') X (D')	(A') X (D')
by Entrepreneur Revenue	r = 0.459*	r = 0.89*
	(p < .05)	(p < .0025)

+ "r" represents Pearson correlation coefficient.
* "r" represents Spearman rank order correlation coefficient for tied observations.
Note: significance levels are one-tailed.

Entrepreneurs were asked to rate various CDC-related experiences or factors on a scale of 1 to 7 depending on how much they thought the experiences contributed to their future entrepreneurial success (1 equals no contribution, 4 equals moderate contribution, 7 equals very strong/exceptional contribution). The factors rated were the following:

1. Formal CDC training
2. CDC management experience
3. CDC technological experience
4. CDC finance/accounting experience
5. Informal contacts maintained with CDC personnel
6. Current business relationship with CDC

Overall, CDC experiences were generally perceived as being quite significant to Canadian and Mexican entrepreneurs (see Table 8). Not surprisingly, however, the Canadians and Mexicans reported differing CDC contributions.

In Canada, CDC technological experience (mean equals 6.0) and managerial experience (mean equals 5.3) were perceived as making a strong contribution to entrepreneurship. All of the Canadian entrepreneurs praised Computing Devices for its long-standing innovative and state-of-the-art operations. From its founding in 1949 and for many years thereafter, Computing Devices was the preeminent electronics firm in the Ottawa area, and it attracted some of the best

Table 8. Entrepreneurs' Assessment of Control Data's Contribution to Their Business Success (1 = no contribution; 4 = moderate; 7 = very strong/exceptional)

Canada

Entre ID #	Formal CDC Training	CDC Management Experience	CDC Tech. Experience	CDC Fin./ Acct. Experience	Informal CDC Contacts	Current Business with CDC
C1	1	5	5.5	1	4	3
C2	2	4	5.5	3.5	4	1
C3*	—	—	—	—	—	—
C4	1	6	—	3	—	1
C5	—	5.5	3.5	5.5	4	1
C6	1	5.5	7	6	5	1
C7	1	4	5.5	1	4	1
C8	1	5.5	6.5	6	4	1
C9	4.5	6	6	5	6	5.5
C10*	—	—	—	—	—	—
C11	2	5	7	6	2	1
C12	—	—	—	—	—	—
C13*	—	—	—	—	—	—
C14	1	5.5	7	4	3	1
C15	1	6	6	5	6	3
C16	—	—	—	—	—	—
Mean =	1.5	5.3	6.0	4.2	4.2	1.8

*did not interview

Mexico

Entre ID #	Formal CDC Training	CDC Management Experience	CDC Tech. Experience	CDC Fin./ Acct. Experience	Informal CDC Contacts	Current Business with CDC
M1 +	5	4	6	3	3	6.5
M2 +	7	5	7	5	1	7
M3	4	2	5	1	1	2
M4 +	4	—	5	1	1	7
M5 +	—	—	—	—	—	—

+ CDC franchisee

Table 8. Continued

Entre ID #	Formal CDC Training	CDC Management Experience	CDC Tech. Experience	CDC Fin./ Acct. Experience	Informal CDC Contacts	Current Business with CDC
M6	5	5	6	5	7	1
M7 +	7	4	7	1	1	7
M8	1	4	5.5	5	6	6
M9	1	7	1	6	7	6
Mean =	4.3	4.4	5.3	3.4	3.4	5.3

Canadian engineers as well as a steady flow of talented British immigrants. This talented core provided a superior foundation for on-the-job technical training comparable to that available at only a few other Canadian locations. This high educational value attributed to the Computing Devices work experience earned it the nickname Bell's Corners Technical College. The informal, on-the-job nature of this training is significant, for although Computing Devices has always provided formal training seminars and classes, the formal training mode was perceived as making a negligible contribution (mean equals 1.6) to entrepreneurial success.

In Mexico, CDC technological experience was perceived as exerting a strong influence (mean equals 5.3) on entrepreneurial success—similar to the Canadian finding. However, in contrast to Canada, CDC's formal training of Mexican entrepreneurs was also considered significant, making a moderate contribution (mean equals 4.3) to entrepreneurial success. This was not unexpected, for six of the nine Mexican entrepreneurs continue to service Control Data computers on which they received substantial, specialized, formal training. Symbolizing the importance of this training, two Mexican entrepreneurs, despite having college degrees, referred to CDC as their "school."

Mexican managers also viewed their managerial background with CDC as contributory (mean equals 4.4) to their current businesses. An entrepreneur elaborates: "They taught me self-administration. They put me on my own with deadlines. I didn't respond at first. I didn't do it. Then I was told, 'you are very important for us, and we need all the information that you will give us because you are very important.' I felt they might be right. They taught me to think like a businessman."

The finance/accounting background obtained at CDC was a final area surveyed regarding the possible transference of tangible skills from corporate employment to subsequent entrepreneurship. In both Canada (mean equals 4.2) and Mexico (mean equals 3.4) these skills were claimed to make a moderate contribution to entrepreneurship. In Canada, former Computing Devices employees were especially laudatory of the subsidiary's cost accounting system, having been developed in the United States and transferred to the Canadian subsidiary. In the Ottawa area, the Computing Devices cost system is today pervasive in the industry, having been implemented in various hybrid forms by many of the former employees who have ventured off to start their own businesses. The testimony of one president/entrepreneur is particularly descriptive:

> It was a good fundamental approach. . . . When I was setting up . . . financial controls in this company, we were only doing about $100,000 worth of business. I set it up so that I knew what we were doing—what our overheads were. They were monitored on a regular basis through a work order system . . . [tracking] project costs. My accountant shook his head and thought I was crazy to be getting that much financial information on an ongoing basis, but it was precisely what allowed me to control projects and to know whether we were making or losing money on a month to month basis . . . [in order] to make corrections before it was too late. . . . This was all very beneficial to the companies that became spinoffs or startups.

Entrepreneurs were also surveyed to ascertain the importance of their continued commercial ties with CDC, either as a purchaser or supplier of products or services. In Canada, business relationships maintained with Computing Devices were few and generally viewed to contribute negligibly (mean equals 1.8) to entrepreneurial success; however, it was revealed that informal contacts maintained with Computing Devices were important (mean equals 4.2) to business, for Computing Devices operates at the hub of an informal regional network that frequently alerts ex-colleagues to commercial opportunities. Furthermore, besides spawning a number of successful entrepreneurs, Computing Devices has proven to be a source of talented employees for the entrepreneurs' firms. Through maintained communication channels, disaffected or frustrated CDC employees are often lured away to join their ex-colleagues' businesses. One particular entrepreneur has filled numerous executive positions with former Computing Devices employees, describing his hiring activities as a "recollection" of former colleagues.

In Mexico, the business relationship maintained between CDC-Mexico and the service franchises, of course, is fundamental to the continued business survival of the entrepreneurs, particularly those most recently started in business. There are indications that this dependent status may subside with time, for most of the more established franchisees have attracted outside revenue sources. Certainly, much will depend on the Mexican economy and its future support for an expanded computer market. In any case, the dependence upon CDC found manifest among franchises appears relatively benign, for CDC-Mexico is likewise reliant upon its franchisees. Their skills are in high demand and not readily replaced in the Mexican labor force.

CDC-Mexico is also active in promoting entrepreneurship through its funding of research and development joint ventures with Mexican partners. This activity is undertaken in part to comply with a government regulation that 5 percent of subsidiary costs must be invested in research and development (R & D).[22] Often falling short of the 5 percent level in direct R & D expenditures, CDC-Mexico frequently makes up some of the disparity through a Mexican university affiliated organization, CETAI, providing it with periodic grants to find potential entrepreneurs who need seed capital to develop new products or processes that are of potential commercial interest to CDC. CDC might choose to fund one from among several projects which CETAI submits for review, investing in the associated entrepreneur and contracting to buy a specific number of finished units for marked up resale. For their investment, CDC typically receives 25 to 40 percent of the new company while CETAI gets 25 to 30 percent. The entrepreneur, for his/her efforts, receives about 40 percent equity in the venture. By these means, CDC actively fosters Mexican entrepreneurship, providing capital to develop uniquely Mexican products. This activity is in congruence with the progressive views of Control Data Corporation's retired founding chairman, William C. Norris, who recognized the innovative capabilities of small business and the utility of technology transfer: "One of the world's largest untapped resources is the wealth of information and technology lying dormant or underutilized in the libraries and laboratories of businesses, governments, research institutes, academic institutions, and individual inventors."[23]

In Canada, CDC has not been as purposefully involved in directly promoting indigenous entrepreneurship, despite the high level of entrepreneurial success manifested by former employees. Nevertheless, in two instances, Canadian entrepreneurs succeeded in initiating their businesses by seizing opportunities created by Computing Devices executives to spin off non-military business segments. One of the resultant spinoff businesses, Dipix, went bankrupt in 1985. The other business actually had corporate sanction for its planned spinoff withdrawn at the 11th hour; however, the would-be director left to form his own company, Senstar, utilizing patented Computing Devices technology to re-create the former business. A lawsuit filed by CDC against this entrepreneur was later resolved in favor of CDC, although an unexpected result was that Senstar purchased the competing Computing Devices' division.

The Dipix spinoff was initiated in 1978, during a period (1977–1978) when Computing Devices was in the trough of its business cycle—the same cycle experienced by large U.S. defense contractors. Diminished revenue motivated the Computing Devices' retrenchment to its core military business, creating the spinoff opportunity.

In addition to the Dipix spinoff, two other enterprises were initiated during the same period by departing employees who were prompted by Computing Devices' cutbacks in non-military business segments.[24] Finally, two other employees left Computing Devices in this time period to become entrepreneurs, claiming to be disenchanted with U.S. corporate heavy-handedness and executive "back stabbing" at Computing Devices—behaviors often associated with lean times in business. Interestingly, the high incidence of entrepreneurship coinciding with Computing Devices' business recession parallels CDC-Mexico's experience, where the franchise concept was implemented pursuant to the period of business downturn.

In both Canada and Mexico, CDC appears to play a strong role in engendering indigenous entrepreneurship. While it remains possible that CDC employment merely served to detain entrepreneurship that would have transpired earlier, objective measures and entrepreneurial testimony have indicated otherwise. Indeed, of the many former CDC employees interviewed, only one in Canada and one in Mexico indicated having had an interest in entrepreneurship prior to CDC employment. For the majority, the decision to initiate a business was made after the opportunity became manifest through unique circumstances. This response pattern supports Glade's hypothesis (see Chapter 2) that entrepreneurial initiative springs from the particular opportunity set with which a capable individual is presented. As the evidence has indicated, the CDC employment experience may have served as the critical activating element in the potential entrepreneurs' opportunity sets.

Whether the "multinational" aspect of CDC is significant to indigenous entrepreneurship is questionable. Findings in this respect bear heavily on judgments regarding the validity of the contending theoretical perspectives, which are sharply at odds concerning the role of the multinational subsidiary.

In Mexico, the state of indigenous technological capabilities precludes the possibility of domestic firms equipping their engineers with backgrounds comparable to that provided by foreign MNCs. In fact, the only existing wholly owned Mexican businesses that produce computer hardware are manufacturers of personal computers; therefore, it seems evident that foreign multinationals play an indispensable role in advancing indigenous technological capabilities. But another bonus to multinational ownership in Mexico may be the diffusion of more efficient managerial practices. Several interviewees cited CDC-Mexico's utilization of performance incentives leading to an employment experience superior to what they believed they would have received if they had been employed by a Mexican owned corporation. Mexican corporations were described as more "political," with friendships and favors dominating the corporate reward and advancement structure.

In Canada, multinational ownership was described as insignificant to the entrepreneurs' employment experience from a technological standpoint, for indigenous Canadian capabilities are already among the more advanced of industrialized nations. Similarly, Canadian management practices are considered relatively efficient, being comparable to U.S. standards. Nevertheless, when queried about the significance of having been employed by a multinational corporation with respect to subsequent business success, the Canadian entrepreneurs showed evidence that a "multinational experience" can be substantive. Of 12 respondents to a question regarding the significance of having been employed by a foreign MNC instead of at a strictly Canadian owned corporation, four claimed they received a distinct benefit from the foreign multinational experience, five claimed no benefit, and three were undecided or indicated they gained only slightly from multinational employment (see Table 9). Upon closer scrutiny, these responses display a striking pattern. It is probably not coincidental that the four respondents who claimed that their multi-

Table 9. Entrepreneurs' Business Data (II)

Canada

Entre ID #	Age at Entre	(E) Years as Entre	MNC Benefit? (yes/no/ undecided)
C1	31	7	no
C2	46	6	yes
C3*	—	—	—
C4	29	7	no
C5	37	17	undecided
C6	43	6	yes
C7	38	10	no
C8	33	9	no
C9	37	6	no
C10*	—	—	—
C11	33	9	undecided
C12	35	17	yes
C13*	—	—	—
C14	36	11	undecided
C15	33	13	yes
C16	33	15	—
Mean =	35.7	10.2	

* did not interview

Mexico

Entre- ID #	Age at Entre	(E) Years as Entre	MNC Benefit? (yes/no/ undecided)
M1 +	30	4	yes
M2 +	33	.75	yes
M3	37	13	yes
M4 +	28	4	yes
M5 +	29	.50	yes
M6	32	3	yes
M7 +	46	4	yes
M8	43	6	yes
M9	51	6	yes
Mean =	36.6	4.6	

+ CDC franchisee

national background was useful were also among the highest ranking
former CDC executives interviewed, each having the status of at
least divisional director.[25] The four engaged in considerable business
travel in their CDC positions, gaining valuable international business
exposure that they claimed helped equip them to succeed abroad as
entrepreneurs who exported an average of 84 percent of their production. The following statement helps illustrate the benefit of Computing Devices' multinational affiliation:

> There was an advantage to me personally in being associated with a
> foreign company. I got some good experience in dealing not just with
> Americans, but with American military procedures and procurement
> procedures and specifications in a way I probably wouldn't have had
> Computing Devices been strictly a Canadian owned company. I would
> have been more parochial and less international. Ultimately, it [i.e., his
> company] became very much an international company. There was no
> domestic market. We had to make it internationally. I would say it [i.e.,
> foreign affiliation] was very beneficial.

Another entrepreneur also elaborates on the benefit of his international background: "In my years with Computing Devices I trav-
elled extensively all over the United States and through Europe with
ASW and remote sensing, providing me worthwhile exposure to international business. This market knowledge helped me very much in
my later business."

The remaining entrepreneurs, of lower managerial rank, had
little or no international business experience with CDC. Not surprisingly, they were far less successful abroad as entrepreneurs, exporting an average of only 32 percent of their production. The ability to
export is often considered very important for business growth, particularly so for Canadian businesses, which often find expansion limited when they are constrained to the small and competitive Canadian market.

In Mexico, a similar pattern emerges. The two highest ranking
former CDC-Mexico employees engaged in considerable international travel (primarily to the United States) in their positions as
president and executive sales manager. They formed the computer
distributorship previously described, and they both extolled the value
of their international experience with CDC, claiming it contributed
to their current successful relationships with the U.S. computer
manufacturers for whom they are distributors.

Considerable evidence of the MNC spread effect was demonstrated by CDC through its Canadian and Mexican subsidiaries. Not only was a significant amount of entrepreneurship undertaken by former employees, but findings indicate that the superior managerial and technological experiences derived by these entrepreneurs during their CDC employ were crucial to the degree of future success they have enjoyed. Furthermore, evidence suggests that the international experience derived from MNC employment may play a critical role in enabling the future entrepreneur to export, expanding his firm's sales and profits.

The spread effect observed in Canada was more visibly pronounced than in Mexico; however, this would be expected given the vastly different economies. In any case, both countries are highly dependent on the U.S. economy; therefore, the indigenous entrepreneurship engendered by CDC represents an important and highly positive aspect of its operations in terms of its contribution to Canadian and Mexican national development goals.

B. Internal Brain Drain

While the spread effect serves to promote indigenous entrepreneurship, the effect of Internal Brain Drain (IBD) is to inhibit it.

IBD is claimed to exert its effect on indigenous entrepreneurship through the MNC subsidiaries' hiring of native employees who would otherwise have become local entrepreneurs. Furthermore, the MNC subsidiary is claimed to be able to retain these employees throughout their careers. The MNC's most prominent critics, the dependencistas, claim that superior salaries cause employee retention, promoting IBD.

To assess CDC's activities in preempting indigenous entrepreneurship through employment, it is important to determine entrepreneurial potential at the time of CDC employment and the ability of CDC salary incentives to deter entrepreneurship.

For these purposes, it is assumed that the answers of interviewed entrepreneurs are representative of other CDC employees—especially including the hypothetical set of employees that may have been deterred from entrepreneurship by CDC employment.

CDC's Canadian and Mexican professionals come to the job with strong academic credentials, usually possessing a technologically oriented, four year degree (typically in electronic engineering). While Canadian professionals are generally more academically advanced than their Mexican counterparts, both groups represent the technological elite of their countries. Thus, from an intellectual standpoint, it is reasonable to surmise that CDC subsidiary employees possess the aptitude for entrepreneurship. Of course, far more than a fine technological education is required for successful entrepreneurship. The value of prior work experience has already been demonstrated. CDC new hires are often quite young and many are inexperienced in business. Among those interviewed, the median age at employment with Computing Devices and CDC-Mexico was 28 and 24 years, respectively. Therefore, for most it is doubtful that entrepreneurship would have been undertaken at such early ages as an alternative to CDC employment. Yet, despite the predominance of youth among CDC new hires, several in both countries did have substantial prior work experience, presumably sufficient for entrepreneurship. For these individuals, it is important to ascertain CDC's role, if any, in deterring entrepreneurship at the time of their employment. Relative to this question, CDC salaries are certainly well above national averages in Canada and Mexico; however, the true significance of salary must be interpreted in the context of industry standards. In the Canadian and Mexican electronic industries, CDC salaries are competitive—about average. In both Canada and Mexico, multinational computer firms and comparable national firms in the computer/electronics industry pay similar salaries. In Mexico, CDC engineers are Mexican citizens and paid according to Mexican standards. For example, among the service engineers, the highest salary was in the $5,000 range—decent at the time, but still modest even by prevailing Mexican criteria. Similar employment with state-owned enterprises is often more lucrative.

In Canada, Computing Devices engineers are unionized and considered well paid, although approximately 20 percent less than their U.S. colleagues. Computing Devices has never been an industry leader in salaries, generally paying on a par with its competition.[26] This has not always been the case. For a period in the mid-1970s, Computing Devices salaries lagged behind industry standards. Employee dissension eventually prompted rectification of the disparity. Another past cause for engineer dissatisfaction was a 15 percent salary gap relative to their public sector equivalents, a condition that persisted through the early 1970s.[27] By that time, most of the future entrepreneurs who were interviewed had already begun their Computing Devices employment, suggesting that salary was not their primary consideration when they made their job choice.[28]

Likewise, in Mexico, the prevalence of superior salaries paid by state-owned enterprises relieves CDC-Mexico from vulnerability to claims of salary-induced preemption of indigenous entrepreneurship. The experience of one interview subject is particularly illustrative. Before he started work on his own he was lured away from CDC-Mexico to a comparable high-level executive position with a state-owned enterprise and was given a substantially greater salary, two government cars, and a personal chauffeur—unheard of perks in Mexican subsidiaries of foreign MNCs.

Canadian and Mexican interview responses offer little evidence of IBD. None of the respondents, when asked about employment alternatives at the time of CDC employment, mentioned considera-tion of self-employment.

Thus, CDC was not found to preempt the entrepreneurial initia-tive of its employees, either at the time of initial employment or subsequently. To the contrary, CDC was seen to have a decidedly positive effect upon indigenous entrepreneurship, providing employ-ees with knowledge and background regarded as superior to that available from most indigenously owned organizations. These entre-preneurs demonstrated considerable success and self-sufficiency and contributed to their nations' development goals.

2. THE DISSUASIVE EFFECT

A. Market Superiority

The multinational subsidiary, by virtue of its inclusion in the greater resource base of the parent company, is more empowered than nonaffiliated organizations of comparable size, as it draws on the parent company for such resources as R & D technology, market research, supply lines, distribution channels, and lobbying efforts. For corporate services rendered, the subsidiary is generally charged a fee based on its proportionate absorption of corporate overhead; however, economies of scale operate to make these services afford-able to the subsidiary, while the unaffiliated organization may find the associated costs prohibitive if it is attempting to create similar capabilities independently. In addition, since the multinational sub-sidiary generally functions as a component of corporate global strat-egy, financial reserves of the parent company are often available, enabling the subsidiary to maintain vital expenditures during periods of cash shortage in accord with a long-term competitive strategy plac-ing greater priority on market share development than on quarterly earnings.

Thus, the MNC subsidiary is eminently capable of competing in foreign industries where some of the aforementioned capabilities are determinants of success. The computer industry serves as an example. It is highly R & D intensive and technologically advanced. In addition, manufacturers' reliance on mercurial international suppliers is high, due to frequent price fluctuations and uncertain delivery times, and those factors favor the larger, multinational corporate structure because it can diversify risk through the utilization of multiple supply sources. Indeed, multinational computer companies from the United States (and to a lesser extent Western Europe and Japan) easily dominate the computer industries in all countries except where they are excluded or severely regulated. In this respect, Computing Devices and CDC-Mexico are representative of the group of U.S. multinational subsidiaries (led by IBM's foreign subsidiaries) which dominates the Canadian and Mexican computer industries.

The inherent technological advantages of multinational computer firms seem to mitigate against the emergence of domestic alternatives in Mexico (except for microcomputers). Only with a concerted industrial policy similar to Brazil's or India's could indigenous firms be expected to start up and survive given the certain superiority of foreign alternatives. In Canada, native technological ability exists for producing state-of-the-art computer hardware. If Canada were denied the products of foreign-based computer manufacturers, indigenous producers would likely arise to service Canadian needs. Nevertheless, given Canada's small domestic market and certain foreign retaliation to instituted trade barriers, the costs of developing an indigenous industry would be exorbitant. Ultimately, increased data processing costs across all industries would be passed on to the Canadian consumer, and the international competitiveness of all Canadian industry would be subject to decline.

Thus, although CDC's subsidiaries may be held partially responsible for hindering the emergence of locally developed substitutes in Canada and Mexico, the overall result for the economies may be favorable. For instance, foreign domination in computer hardware provides Canadian and Mexican entrepreneurs with incentive to produce associated products and services (e.g., printed circuit boards, peripherals, software, computing devices) for which they may possess a comparative advantage. For example, more advanced developing countries would appear to have a comparative advantage in the production of computer software, which Karl P. Sauvant claims is based upon their good supply of technically trained, low cost labor.

Compared to the cost of a U.S. computer professional—which ranges between $60,000 and $140,000 per person—software professionals in a developing country cost between $18,000 and $25,000 per year. This figure includes salary, benefits, and direct and indirect costs such as space, communications, utilization, and management overhead. . . . A number of developing countries possess an educational infrastructure capable of training first-rate data processing engineers and computer scientists. . . . Within Latin America, Argentina, Brazil, Mexico, and Venezuela have the largest training capability; as a result, these four countries are particularly favored for developing an internationally competitive software industry.[29]

However, given the severity of their computer policies, Sauvant argues that Brazil and India would probably face great problems in developing internationally competitive software, having cut off their access to certain state-of-the-art hardware and systems software as a result of their indigenization drives. These import barriers

limit their capability to develop new products because the industry cannot respond sufficiently fast to hardware changes to compete in state-of-the-art software markets in developed market economies. Among the products sold in these markets are standard packages that must be tailored to new system configurations, as well as new software developments that must cater to the rapidly changing technological environments (for example, new versions of compilers, data-base systems, data-communications protocols, and terminals).[30]

In contrast to Brazil and India, Mexico has an advantage in the development of applications software for export, because it has access to state-of-the-art hardware and systems software that enable it to compete in international markets.[31] Mexico's advantage, of course, comes from its relatively greater openness to the multinational computer firm. It was previously mentioned that the two most successful entrepreneurs among former CDC employees have recently succeeded in exporting their software to PepsiCo, Inc., in Guatemala—software compatible with Hewlett-Packard (U.S.) hardware. These entrepreneurs are attempting to turn their business in the direction of software development, for which they seem to have recognized their country's comparative advantage in producing internationally competitive software products.

In Canada, several of the entrepreneurs produce electronic devices for integration into U.S.-designed state-of-the-art computer systems. As exports to the U.S. market represent a sizable fraction of the entrepreneurial revenue of former Computing Devices employees interviewed, the consequence of Canadian computer hardware industry being dominated by U.S. multinationals is beneficial, facilitating their products' compatibility with U.S. consumer systems.

While MNC dominance of the Canadian and Mexican computer industries accounts for the absence of indigenous substitutes, it is improbable that this state of affairs inhibits indigenous entrepreneurship. A decision to exclude U.S. computer products in Canada or Mexico would necessitate a mobilization of scarce national resources to create an indigenous industry that would likely be technologically inferior (in Mexico's case) or less cost efficient (in Canada's case)—as Brazil and India have demonstrated. Furthermore, the indigenous entrepreneurship in computer hardware that would emerge to replace MNC production would be counterbalanced to an extent by the entrepreneurship stifled, not only among potential software exporters, but also among all industrial exporters for whom information processing and analysis costs are significant.

B. Capital Availability

Its critics claim that the MNC subsidiary is especially adept at attracting investment capital from local financial institutions and venture capitalists, greatly depleting the supply available for indigenous entrepreneurs and thereby suppressing the level of local business formation and expansion.

Computing Devices was purchased in 1969 by Control Data Corporation from the Bendix Corporation for more than $20 million—the lion's share financed by loans from Canadian banks.

In assessing the effect of this loan, it is probably not fair to say that this amount was diverted from *potential* entrepreneurs, for new entrepreneurs are not typically considered in the risk category to which commercial banks extend loans. Even in times of abundant capital, banks generally lend money only to those small businessmen who have demonstrated track records. Otherwise, some may view the loan as having been diverted from *existing* Canadian entrepreneurs; however, such a diversion would have been temporary, for Computing Devices' particular debt was paid off in its entirety (with interest) in 1980—replenishing available Canadian loan capital.

As for equity investment, Computing Devices is 100 percent

owned by CDC-U.S; thus, local equity capital supplies were not affected.

Similarly, CDC-Mexico is a 100-percent-owned subsidiary of CDC-U.S. CDC-Mexico was established in 1965 at the request of a potential Mexican customer who wanted assurances that CDC was committed to servicing its computers. Initially employing only three, CDC-Mexico operated almost exclusively as a sales and servicing office in its early years. CDC-Mexico had few assets or capital needs, thus it did not diminish the supply of local investment capital. Its current size has been attained primarily through reinvested earnings.

In summary, for both CDC's subsidiaries, equity investment was entirely U.S.-sourced, while debt financing in the Canadian case was serviced and repaid within 11 years. Thus, CDC's activities in Canada and Mexico do not demonstrate a diversion of capital from local entrepreneurs. This is a conservative analysis, based on the assumption of capital scarcity, previously suggested to be questionable.

Entrepreneurial Displacement

1. DISPLACEMENT THROUGH PURCHASE

It is recognized that the purchase of indigenous businesses was a common means of entry for multinational corporations in their establishment of foreign subsidiaries during the postwar decades. More recently, however, this activity has subsided somewhat. While buyouts of domestic businesses continue to occur with regularity, a significant fraction of this activity is today attributable to foreign MNCs purchasing the subsidiaries of other foreign MNCs.

CDC's activities in Canada and Mexico reflect contemporary trends. CDC has never bought out an indigenously owned business in Canada or Mexico, either at the time the subsidiary was established or during the course of operations.

Computing Devices itself, however, was originally a Canadian-owned corporation whose entrepreneurs had been displaced through foreign purchase. Circumstances associated with the purchase, however, reflect favorably upon the role of foreign capital.

To elaborate, prior to its purchase by CDC, Computing Devices was a subsidiary of Bendix and also operated as CDC's marketing representative in Canada. Bendix had gained virtual control over Computing Devices in 1956 (formalized in 1962) through stock purchases from the founding Canadian entrepreneurs. The sale to Bendix was actively sought by the Canadian owners of Computing

Devices, who claimed to be unable to raise the additional funds within Canada.[32] The situation was indeed critical, for additional financing at the time was believed to be essential in order for Computing Devices to avoid bankruptcy. As one Computing Devices executive put it, "there comes a time when every company reaches a point where it can either expand or grow, or sink if no finances are available."[33] Thus, rather than operating to extinguish indigenous entrepreneurship, multinational investment served as a savior, infusing the necessary resources for survival and growth and enabling Computing Devices to become a training base for a host of future Canadian entrepreneurs.

2. DISPLACEMENT THROUGH COMPETITION

In Canada and Mexico, no evidence of CDC driving existing indigenous entrepreneurs out of business was revealed by the methodology employed. The field of consideration was admittedly small, for multinational dominance in computers (except personal computers) is almost complete in both countries—leaving few existing competitors to consider. Nevertheless, indigenous competition does exist for other CDC products.

In the few observed instances of CDC and indigenous businesses competing head to head, indigenous businesses demonstrated considerable staying power. In the Canadian case previously highlighted, Senstar has proven to be a formidable competitor for Computing Devices, and, most notably, has recently purchased the competing Computing Devices division.

In Mexico, CDC's line of minicomputers (its major source of hardware revenue in the country) is losing sales to microcomputer manufacturers, due to performance and storage enhancements in the smaller product lines. Some of these sales have been lost to Intelecsis and Datamex, Mexican-owned firms.

Overall, as no evidence of competitive displacement was discovered, it is concluded that CDC's competitive effect is largely positive, in that it serves to stimulate industrial efficiency as indigenous competitors rationalize their managerial and manufacturing processes, benefitting from the diffusion of the multinational corporation's know-how.

Summary

The effects of CDC's influence upon indigenous entrepreneur-ship were found to be consistently positive and in strong support of modernization theory. In both Canada and Mexico, CDC's advanced technological capabilities and managerial practices were shown to provide its employees with a background that fostered their later entrepreneurial success. Significantly, the incidence and success of entrepreneurship was most visibly pronounced in Canada. Further-more, the character of the entrepreneurship was found to be highly complementary to national development goals that seek to achieve lessened dependence on the U.S. economy. Toward this goal, the Canadian entrepreneurs have been very successful; they maintain minimal business connections with Computing Devices and export almost three-quarters of their production. Mexican entrepreneurs are more dependent upon CDC, although trends reveal a lessening of dependence over time, as new entrepreneurs utilize their base of CDC support as a platform to venture into more independent com-merce.

In further support of CDC's positive role for indigenous entre-preneurs, little evidence of preemption of potential entrepreneurs and displacement of existing entrepreneurs was discovered. For in-stance, CDC salaries have never exceeded industry norms and have even lagged at times, demonstrating no special ability of CDC to divert or preempt potential entrepreneurs through employment. Likewise, CDC was not found to hinder indigenous entrepreneurship by depleting common sources of small business funding, because it never relied on venture capital or other Canadian or Mexican equity markets. In fact, equity financing was raised entirely in the United States, while debt, in the Canadian case, was quickly repaid and thus recycled. In addition, CDC was not found to pose a threat to already established indigenous entrepreneurs. In fact, CDC has never bought out an existing locally owned business in Canada or Mexico. Further-more, there is no evidence that CDC's business success has forced indigenous competitors to fold. The case of Senstar in Canada demon-strates the competitive mettle of former employees turned entrepre-neur.

The significance of these results involves the extent to which CDC's effects upon indigenous entrepreneurship may be considered comparable to those of other multinational firms in the high technology industries—industries whose indigenous development is considered by MNC critics to be critical to the future progress and greater autonomy of the dependent countries.

One of CDC's outstanding contributions to Canadian entrepreneurship concerned its subsidiary's incorporation into a large international network. Business experience with CDC in the international arena was characteristic of those entrepreneurs who distinguished themselves as the most successful of former Computing Devices employees, aiding their exporting efforts. It is suggested that multinational affiliation can provide departing indigenous executives with the capabilities to excel in business when the nature of the their endeavor requires export sales to be competitive. This is certainly true among LDCs and among smaller advanced industrialized countries (AICs), which generally lack a sufficient home market in the areas of production in which high technology firms specialize. CDC's activities in Canada are of a type that is common among MNCs. Computing Devices' state-of-the-art operations, its extensive international ties, and its reluctance to purchase indigenous firms are features prevalent among high technology subsidiaries of MNCs from AICs.

In Mexico, except in the case of the two computer distributors, CDC's international business operations were not significant to its future entrepreneurs, for their businesses were targeted to the Mexican domestic market. However, CDC's superior technological capabilities and managerial practices were found to make significant contributions to entrepreneurial success. These advantages may be considered characteristic of most MNCs operating in less developed host countries—especially the case for high technology subsidiaries, where local deficiencies are comparatively most pronounced. In addition, in high technology areas, MNCs are least onerous to local businesses, for they generally are not in competition with each other. Thus, entrepreneurial displacement would be relatively absent, while diffusion of scarce capabilities to indigenous employees would be maximized.

Otherwise, CDC-Mexico is most unique in its franchising operations. Eleven of 14 entrepreneurs are franchisees, and although these activities currently generate only a small fraction of entrepreneurial revenue, they are of recent establishment and merit scrutiny as models for future national efforts to promote indigenous entrepreneurship through the MNC subsidiary.

In conclusion, the analysis of CDC's international operations has disclosed conditions where MNC subsidiaries from advanced industrialized countries offer distinct opportunities to benefit indigenous entrepreneurship in dependent countries. Through its employment of indigenous professionals and managers, the MNC subsidiary transmits knowledge and experiences that are less available locally. This is particularly the case in industries most dominated by foreign capital, where local capabilities are most deficient. By diffusing its special capabilities through employment, MNC subsidiaries equip future entrepreneurs to engage in a variety of new indigenous businesses, if not in direct competition with their former employers, then in associated areas in which their initially smaller enterprises have a natural competitive advantage. The result of a rising incidence of indigenous entrepreneurship is diminishing dependence, a foremost goal among affected nations.

CHAPTER 6

State Policy and Entrepreneurship

In light of the shortage of private industrial entrepreneurship in Canada, Mexico, and other dependent or less developed countries, the results of this study provide policymakers with encouragement and justification for opening up their economies to greater levels of foreign direct investment—foregoing recourse to a bargaining or dependency/nationalization strategy. In considering Canada's and Mexico's standing with respect to the ideal, a review of the policies that both governments direct toward fdi in their computer industries is presented, for these policies affect the level and character of multinational activity, delimiting the potential benefit to indigenous entrepreneurship.

Mexican Computer Policy

In comparison to Brazil's and India's more interventionist and insulating policies, Mexican computer policies are less onerous to fdi and also less rigidly enforced. Significantly, Mexican policies recognize the country's need to rely on foreign technology throughout the computer industry. Mexican computer policies are still significantly restrictive, certainly more so than in the newly industrialized countries of the Far East.

THE MEXICAN COMPUTER DECREE

Although Mexico has been using computers since the early 1960s, its market was completely supplied by imports prior to 1981, when the government instituted a formal decree regulating the manufacture and trade of computers and peripherals.[1] The new policies have produced significant results, enabling Mexico to produce its own computers with the assistance of foreign capital and technology. In this manner, the need to import finished computer systems and components has been reduced, and Mexico hopes gradually to increase its technological capabilities with the assistance of foreign companies to become a leading microcomputer exporter.[2]

A survey of the decree's general provisions follows.

Local Manufacturing and Equity Requirements

With respect to computer systems, the decree limits its purview to micro- and minicomputers. Foreign microcomputer manufacturers are statutorily prohibited from importing their finished wares. In order to sell to the Mexican market, they are required to manufacture locally and are limited to a 49 percent equity share in the associated company. IBM is a significant exception, as it is allowed to own its Mexican microcomputer manufacturing operations entirely.[3]

Mexico's 49 percent equity limitation is more often relaxed with respect to minicomputers, an acknowledgment of the shortage of Mexican businessmen capable of starting up such technologically advanced operations. Hewlett-Packard, for example, produces its 3000 series minicomputer in Guadalajara at a wholly owned subsidiary; IBM likewise produces minis in Mexico at a wholly owned subsidiary.[4] Similarly, CDC-Mexico is wholly owned by its U.S. parent and does not manufacture minicomputers in Mexico. Describing this favorable treatment, a CDC-Mexico executive explained, "all laws in Mexico are subject to different interpretation."

Domestic Content Requirements

The computer decree contains domestic content requirements that aim to increase the reliance of MNC producers upon locally produced inputs, thereby lessening the national import bill and the associated demand for precious foreign exchange. Domestic content requirements were designed to be phased in gradually and were originally to cover 70 percent of market demand by 1988 (up from 30 percent in 1983).[5]

Deficiencies in local capabilities have necessitated nonenforcement of compliance to the mandated levels. For example, CDC-Mexico has not had to adhere to domestic content requirements, importing virtually all of its minicomputer hardware. Nevertheless, some progress in domestic content has been made by CDC-Mexico, for many of its computer systems today contain locally produced terminals, software, and memory add-ons.

Export Requirements

In order to expand its debt servicing capability, Mexico hopes to generate greater foreign exchange from exports of manufactured computers. To fulfill this goal, computer firms are required to increase their ratio of exports to imports gradually. By the fifth year of operation, foreign minicomputer vendors are required to fulfill a 1-to-1 ratio of exports to imports and compensate for any shortfall by paying a penalty of equal value.[6] This policy is claimed to be well-enforced and to have achieved considerable success. In the computer sector, "Mexico exports 50 cents for every dollar imported [in 1985], up from two cents in 1981."[7]

A firm's export requirements are often achieved through indirect means. For instance, CDC-Mexico does not actually export any of its computers. Alternatively, its export requirement is met through export credits purchased from surplus vendors and through joint ventures with maquiladora businesses and local producers of exported multilayered circuit boards.[8]

Research and Development Requirements

Computer firms in Mexico are obligated to spend between 5 and 6 percent of the value of subsidiary sales on research and development,[9] a requirement enacted with the goal of enhancing indigenous technological capabilities. Debra Miller explains that the R & D obligation can be fulfilled through indirect means.

> Various activities qualify as R & D expenditures, from developing a new system or part of one at an approved Mexican research center or at a Mexican plant, the development of machinery and equipment for testing, to the adaptation of a purchased system. The government has approved several facilities where firms can find computer R & D, including the Monterrey Institute of Technology, UNAM, and Unitech.[10]

CDC-Mexico, in addition to its standard in-house R & D expenditures,[11] funds a fraction of its R & D requirements through CETAI (see Chapter 5), an organization affiliated with the Universidad Nacional Autónoma de Mexico. The computer decree also calls for the multinational parent company's most advanced technology to be made available to its Mexican subsidiaries.[12] Summarizing the R & D provisions of the computer decree, Miller concludes that

> overall [they] are consistently enforced. . . . The larger companies, such as IBM and Xerox, are quite proud of their efforts to aid Mexican technological development. For example, IBM is helping the Mexicans

to produce multi-layered circuitized packaging, and to learn semi-conductor design, as well as demonstrating how to provide vendor support.[13]

Incentives

While all the above described elements of the decree restrict foreign investors' felixibility, the decree also established incentives to attract foreign manufacturing investment, including various tax credits and price discounts on energy usage.[14] Since 1985, however, most of the incentives have been rescinded, with Mexico yielding to U.S. claims that these were tantamount to subsidies under the General Agreement on Tariffs and Trade (GATT) code, conferring an unfair advantage in international trade to Mexican computer producers.

Nevertheless, the Mexican government does still provide local manufacturers with some limited support in the form of tax credits and grants; however, according to CDC executives, this aid is very uncoordinated, too discretionary, and lacks a coherent strategy. Similar support exists for indigenously owned software developers; however, the former CDC employees who now develop their own software indicated that they have not sought assistance, for the funds are modest and difficult to obtain and do not justify the costs associated with the application process.

Summary of the Computer Decree

The computer decree has achieved its goal of stimulating the local manufacture of computers. While Mexico has allowed the industry to remain reliant on foreign investment and technology, it has made considerable progress toward increasing the percent of Mexican value-added in the industry. Mexican-owned manufacturing firms have been able to produce terminals, software, printers, and even microcomputers, achieving a degree of self-reliance in these areas. This new entrepreneurship conforms with national development goals; however, the Mexican computer market and industry have not grown as hoped, reflecting the country's continued economic problems. To stimulate the economy, greater levels of new fdi are being sought and policies are being reconsidered and revised. Mexico's lowering of its tariff barriers to imports may prove to be a telling test of the computer decree's lasting benefits through observations of whether unprotected indigenously owned businesses and local multinational manufacturers can rise to meet international competition.

If successful, these producers will demonstrate the utility of an "infant industry" strategy, as government support provided during the industry's early years is withdrawn with the aim that local producers will later advance sufficiently to compete successfully with imports. On the other hand, a failure of local producers to thrive when less protected from import competition would call into question the wisdom of the original computer decree and demonstrate government's difficulty in picking "winners"—a basic requirement of an "infant industry" strategy. Early indications are that indigenously owned producers will be hard-pressed. For example, Mexican microcomputers cost 50 percent more than foreign imports,[15] generating great doubt that indigenously owned producers can cut costs sufficiently to survive without continued protection. In addition, lower tariffs will cause multinational manufacturers in Mexico to lose much of their incentive for local production; however, future expected growth of the Mexican market may offer compensating rewards to continued local manufacturing such as shortened delivery times and greater servicing capabilities.

Canadian Computer Policy

In contrast to Mexico, Canada has not directly targeted its computer industry with an industrial policy regulating foreign direct investment. Otherwise, all new fdi entering Canada, irrespective of industry, is subject to review under the general provisions of Investment Canada, the national fdi review agency. As a general rule, Investment Canada welcomes new fdi, with certain exceptions according to industry.[16] In the Canadian computer industry, multinational subsidiaries and indigenously owned businesses receive relatively equal treatment under the law. Consequently, computer MNCs have not been prevented from prospering and, as indicated by Computing Devices' experience, from contributing to indigenous entrepreneurship.

Numerous financial incentives are available to indigenous and foreign-owned Canadian computer firms, enhancing their prospects for commercial success. These incentives are designed to stimulate innovation and technological advancement in Canadian industry. Funds are generally provided in the form of grants and low interest loans to support promising business projects and through tax credits for qualifying research and development expenditures. While these programs do not directly target the computer industry, the highly

R & D-intensive nature of the industry makes the incentives particularly attractive. The more significant programs are described below; some were utilized by several former CDC employees in their subsequent entrepreneurship:

INDUSTRIAL RESEARCH AND DEVELOPMENT INCENTIVES ACT (IRDIA), EXPIRED

IRDIA provided subsidies for Canadian corporations (foreign or indigenously owned) based upon their domestic R & D spending. Subsidies were equal to

a) 25 percent of the fiscal year increase in R & D spending over the previous five year average.
b) 25 percent of capital expenditures for R & D facilities in the fiscal year.

Initially, the subsidies were awarded retrospectively but later were available in advance based upon proposed expenditures.

From its establishment, many in government circles did not consider this program to be sharply enough focused, resulting in the establishment of PAIT, next described.[17]

PROGRAM FOR THE ADVANCEMENT OF INDUSTRIAL TECHNOLOGY (PAIT), EXPIRED

The basic purpose of PAIT was to increase growth and efficiency of Canadian manufacturing and processing industries by providing financial assistance to companies on a selective basis for the development of new and better products and processes with which to serve larger markets.

Through 1970, the program received little industrial response, due to a payback requirement of principal and interest in the event of project success. The program later expanded from $12.7 million to $51.1 million when the payback provision was rescinded. In 1977, however, the program was replaced by the Enterprise Development Program (EDP), established to combat the widespread belief that Canadian business was deteriorating in international competitiveness.[18]

ENTERPRISE DEVELOPMENT PROGRAM (EDP)

EDP was designed with the priority of enhancing Canada's international competitiveness through focussing financial assistance (grants and subsidized loans) on small- and medium-sized firms engaged in innovative activity in Canada. In addition, the concept of incrementality was an explicit program objective, meaning that subsidies were to be directed to induce firms to undertake worthwhile projects that would not otherwise be undertaken due to their inherent riskiness.[19]

INDUSTRIAL RESEARCH ASSISTANCE PROGRAM (IRAP), EST. 1962

Canadian companies that undertake R & D investment in "production activities based on the physical and biological sciences and engineering ... are eligible for IRAP grants ... [which] pay staff salary costs."[20]

Two of the interviewed entrepreneurs claimed to have received significant benefits from IRAP grants, providing them with salary support for certain personnel during their earlier years of business.

DEFENSE INDUSTRY PRODUCTIVITY PROGRAM (DIPP), EST. 1959

DIPP encourages R & D investment into product and process development in the defense industries. Assistance is given in the form of grants and repayable loans on a shared-cost basis. Generally, about 50 percent of the total cost of the selected R & D is covered.[21]

Only one of the interviewed entrepreneurs received assistance from DIPP. To obtain funds from DIPP and other programs, his business employs an individual whose sole function is to locate and apply for government assistance. Another entrepreneur who indicated an awareness of DIPP expressed a reluctance to apply for government assistance, claiming that "the perceived headache was not worth the benefit."

PROGRAM FOR INDUSTRY/LABORATORY PROJECTS (PILP), EST. 1975

PILP is designed to promote the transfer of Canadian federal laboratory results to Canadian companies (foreign or indigenously owned) in order to develop product and process innovations. Funds are provided through the negotiation of license contracts or through a contribution arrangement with Canadian companies.[22]

Only one of the entrepreneurs received assistance from PILP; however, this individual claimed that the government license obtained through the program was the sole reason for his company's existence—having grown to $90 million in sales in 1987. Despite benefitting from the award of a government license, the entrepreneur echoed the sentiments of some nonapplicants:

> Dealing with the government is always a first class pain in the neck, so, given that, we adopted the policy and practice early in the game of saying we are not going to beat them, they are our friends, let's work with them, find out what they need, and let's give it to them, and let's not fight it every inch of the way. So we did and we didn't really have any problems. We worked hard and encouraged our scientists . . . [to make] a practice of giving the credit to the NRC [National Research Council].

THE TECHNICAL INFORMATION SERVICE (TIS), EST. 1945

The TIS was established by the National Research Council to make current technology available to Canadian industry and to assist industry in the application of the technology. Through TIS, industry is furnished access to NRC's laboratories and libraries and provided with technological information and/or direct technical assistance from NRC's scientists and engineers.

In a reivew of Canadian programs directed toward promoting innovation, Abraham Tarasofsky indicates that TIS has directed its services toward "the overwhelming proportion of Canadian manufacturing enterprises that have little or no in-house capabilities and whose management, for one reason or another, is not familiar with the current technological developments and literature that could be relevant for their operations."[23]

None of the entrepreneurs who were interviewed availed themselves of TIS's services since they were already technologically proficient because of their engineering backgrounds.

TAX CREDITS

Since the 1960s Canada has provided tax credits for the purpose of stimulating R & D capital formation. In 1983, the rates for eligible expenses were increased to 35 percent for companies subject to the small business income tax.[24]

Most of the interviewed entrepreneurs indicated having taken advantage of the tax credits, more popular than the grant and loan programs due to their noncompetitive availability and the avoidance of an application process.

The reviewed grant and tax incentive programs both stimulate

Canadian innovative activity and are available to all eligible Canadian companies, irrespective of national ownership. Thus, in the Canadian computer industry, fdi is not competitively disadvantaged with respect to government incentive programs, an advantageous feature when considering fdi's potential for benefitting indigenous entrepreneurship.

Otherwise, the net economic benefit of these government programs to Canada is uncertain. While R & D investment has been found to account for some 20 to 60 percent of the growth of Canadian productivity,[25] it is questionable whether the incremental R & D expenditures undertaken in response to government incentive programs are similarly productive or instead manifest diminishing returns. In considering this possibility, Canadian R & D expenditures as a percent of its GDP are consistently less than the average for OECD nations,[26] suggesting that greater R & D is necessary and would be productively spent. However, the R & D spending level may be a misleading statistic due to the special contribution of foreign-controlled firms, which are relatively abundant in Canada. Foreign-controlled firms tend to be less R & D intensive than their Canadian owned competitors;[27] however, Donald McFetridge has noted that this deficiency is often counteracted by their serving "as an outlet for their parent companies' innovative technologies," providing "a conduit through which new and sophisticated technology that is relatively expensive to develop enters Canada."[28] In this manner, Canadian industry may receive "free rider" benefits from foreign technology transfer, a process that would be especially pronounced in the Canadian computer industry, where foreign firms are highly concentrated. Thus, despite low R & D intensity, many Canadian industries exhibit high technological intensity overall, owing to their foreign affiliation. In such cases, government incentive programs may be suboptimal, causing MNCs to "overspend" locally for R & D, since similar technology could have been produced more cheaply abroad and transferred to the Canadian subsidiary without the added public cost.

In addition, since the financial incentives from all of the cited programs except TIS and the R & D tax credit are competitively awarded, the competitive relations between firms are altered, potentially harming the prospects for nonsubsidized firms. For example, the discriminatory nature of government subsidies was claimed by an affected owner to have contributed to the failure of his business, the only one which went bankrupt from among those owned by the entrepreneurs who were interviewed. In the particular case, a major competitor had been tagged by the Canadian government as a "Center of Excellence." The entrepreneur explained that

> in Canada, the Canadian government recognizes, and rightly so, that the Canadian market is not all that big. Consequently, companies in Canada, in order to compete on an international scale have to be sort of pampered and in certain business areas are tagged as "centers of excellence." The net result of being tagged is that it becomes easier for you to get government support; grant applications become easier. However, if someone else is tagged as a "COE" and you're trying to buck him, its a helluva lot tougher. Therefore, since [our competitor] was a "COE" we didn't apply for any government support grants for the first two years, and decided we wouldn't go after any major grants until we got established.

Discriminatory incentives rely on government's ability to "pick winners" or properly designate "COEs." If government makes an inappropriate designation, otherwise superior competitors may be forced out of business. Similarly, innovative entrepreneurs may be inhibited from undertaking new business in industries where subsidized COEs are advantaged. These possible effects cast doubt on the wisdom of Canadian policy, suggesting the uncertain results may not justify the diversion of tax dollars and the discriminatory departure from free market principles.

Together, the reviewed policies of Canada and Mexico toward fdi in the computer industry illustrate quite different approaches.

Canada has had no specific industrial policy toward its computer industry. In addition, foreign computer firms in Canada are generally accorded equal access to public incentives for innovative activity, heightening the stimulus for MNC investment. On the other hand, through regulations restricting MNC investment, Mexican industrial policy has attempted to provoke the development of indigenously controlled computer firms. Overall, however, Mexican computer policy has had an uncertain effect on fdi. While high tariffs on computer imports have motivated certain foreign manufacturers to locate their operations in Mexico, non-manufacturing sales and service subsidiaries have often been excluded. Whatever its overall effect upon fdi, the computer decree has been judged to be insufficient for promoting future growth in Mexico. Increasingly liberal enforcement of the computer decree has signaled Mexico's keen interest in attracting an acceleration in foreign direct investment in the sector.

In any case, increases in foreign direct investment do not automatically provoke increased entrepreneurial activity, and for Canada, a sustained high level of MNC subsidiary infiltration into Canadian industry has not been associated with high levels of indigenous entrepreneurship. Influenced by this knowledge, many MNC critics conclude that foreign direct investment is inherently counterproductive to national development goals. But this conclusion is misinformed, for much of indigenous entrepreneurship's responsiveness to fdi depends upon the character of the broad institutional environment to which the investment is introduced. Often in dependent countries, a predominance of import substitution industrialization (I-S-I) policies prove to be the primary cause for high fdi concentration. In these instances, MNC subsidiaries respond to the characteristically high tariff barriers of an I-S-I strategy by manufacturing in the host country, avoiding prohibitive import tariffs. In addition, and more harmfully, the foreign subsidiaries are often further enticed by insulation from external competition and lured with financial incentives (e.g., tax holidays), enabling monopolization of the host market and causing a parallel submergence of indigenous entrepreneurship. In such instances, the high level of fdi and the low level of indigenous entrepreneurship are both shaped by I-S-I policies, exerting their deleterious effect through conditioning the entire economic environment in which businesses operate. Through market distortions created by their anticompetitive orientation, I-S-I policies overwhelm many of the potential benefits of fdi, instead depressing indigenous enterprise and economic development.

In addition to the stagnating I-S-I policies, other inefficient institutional structures characterize Canada and Mexico, further subverting private industrial entrepreneurship. In both countries, businesses and individuals are overtaxed, overregulated, unevenly subsidized, and in competition with government for financial capital and market share.

In Canada, overall rates of taxation are estimated to be 9 to 10 percent higher than in the United States, extinguishing much of the incentive to do business. For individual Canadian taxpayers, tax freedom day has arrived at a progressively later date in recent years—July 10 for 1988.[29] In Mexico, the highest tax rate (40 percent) is levied on incomes as low as $13,170, considered excessive by international standards.[30] Despite heavy taxation, the public sectors of Canada and Mexico are heavily burdened with debt that causes the diversion of resources from private domestic hands. Mexico's plight is the more pronounced, with 60 percent of its 1989 federal budget devoted to debt servicing.[31] Strained to maintain public services and to support an often corrupt and inefficient contingent of publicly owned enterprises, the Mexican government until recently has been engaged in super-inflationary policies, deteriorating the value of its currency and the confidence of indigenous investors, who have expatriated an estimated $40 to $50 billion since 1982.[32]

The case of Petróleos Mexicanos (PEMEX), Mexico's publicly owned petrochemical monopoly and largest corporation, illustrates the corruption and inefficiencies plaguing many publicly owned enterprises in Mexico. In 1983, PEMEX was about 15 times the size of the second largest Mexican state enterprise.[33] Mexico's expenditures on PEMEX account for 20 to 25 percent of the annual federal budget, and although PEMEX concessions provide the Mexican state with 40 percent of its annual revenue and export earnings,[34] PEMEX is among the most corrupt of publicly owned companies in Mexico. Company officials and union bosses, by means catalogued in the international press,[35] have managed to amass private fortunes through their PEMEX affiliation. PEMEX's corruption is truly grand in scale, resulting in operations whose efficiency has been estimated to be only one-fifth that of Royal Dutch Shell.[36] Many PEMEX union leaders are regionally entrenched as quasi-political leaders, receiving the base of their support from a loyal constituency of relatively overpaid labor, whose ranks are claimed to overstaff PEMEX by an estimated 30 percent.[37]

With oil-rich PEMEX in the forefront, the scope of Mexico's entire public sector expanded from 1970 through 1982, as state-controlled companies swelled in number from 39 to 677.[38] Public sector expansion was accompanied by a proliferation of regulations hostile to fdi. Passed in conformity with the populist policies of President Luis Echeverría, the 1973 Law to Promote Mexican Investment and Regulate Foreign Investment put into action a Mexicanization process which Dale Story claims to be responsible for reducing the role of foreign capital over the next ten years:

> Specifically, very few foreign-dominated firms have been established, and many have reverted to Mexican control, either public or private.... From 1973 to 1982 only 44 new enterprises (with the excep-

tion of 240 maquiladora establishments) were created with more than
49 percent foreign participation, whereas 1,987 new firms had less
than 49 percent foreign investment. In addition to the small number
of new firms with foreign control, 498 existing firms had been Mexican-
ized by 1982 under the 1973 Foreign Investment Law.[39]

The restrictions on foreign investment created an initial decline
in fdi's contribution to total Mexican industrial production, which fell
to 28.1 percent in 1975 from a 1970 high of 32.4 percent.[40] During
this time, the Mexican private sector was unable to increase its own
share to compensate for the foreign rollback. Alternatively, state enterprise increased its share by 4.9 percent, more than replacing the
MNC decline.[41]

Other significant regulations enacted during the Echeverría tenure were the 1973 Law on Transfer of Technology and the 1976 Law
on Patents and Trademarks.[42] Both threatened the foreign MNCs'
sense of security regarding the stability of their intellectual property
rights, further dissuading foreign investment. As a result of fdi's lesser
representation in the Mexican economy, indigenous business was deprived of benefits that would have accrued from the transfer of technology, management training, efficiency stimulating competition, and
commercial linkages to indigenous suppliers.

In Canada, regulations on foreign investment were instituted in
1975 with the establishment of a review procedure, administered by
the Foreign Investment Review Agency (FIRA), for the purpose of
evaluating new foreign investment or changes in foreign ownership
in terms of the contribution to "Canadian interests."[43] In contrast to
its Mexican counterpart, FIRA was not especially restrictive of fdi
in most industries, and the book value of total inward investment
increased from $36.4 billion to $54.2 billion between 1974 and
1979,[44] an 8.3 percent rate of growth—comparable to pre-FIRA levels. In 1984, FIRA was renamed Investment Canada, reflecting the
more actively receptive attitude to fdi embodied by the current Conservative government, with the charge to encourage the location of
foreign investment in Canada.[45]

Yet in Canada, despite fdi's continued strong presence, indigenous entrepreneurship has not flourished, as it is suppressed by a tax
system that is one of the world's most burdensome and by an over-
reaching public sector that diverts capital from private use.[46]

Fortunately, more recent developments in Canada offer hope for
indigenous entrepreneurs. The 1988 Free Trade Agreement with the

United States promises to phase out all mutual tariffs over a ten-year period. This action should stimulate greater productivity and export capability among less-protected indigenously owned enterprises boosted by cheaper imported inputs and activated by the challenge of foreign competition.

In addition, government-owned companies in Canada are being privatized in increasing numbers, reflecting a worldwide trend acknowledging the inefficiencies associated with government ownership. These privatizations serve to free capital for private use, establishing easier commercial credit and, thus, greater incentives for entrepreneurship. Already, the Canadian federal government "has sold off a majority of Air Canada and all of the state's holding in two aircraft makers and a telecommunications concern."[47]

Mexico's problems are far more formidable. It is of interest that Mexican entrepreneurship is known to thrive in the underground economy, which is estimated to account for as much as a 33 percent understatement of true GDP.[48] On the other hand, Marvin Alisky has described why entrepreneurship in the regulated industrial sector is sadly lacking:

> in Mexico, a labyrinth of regulations encourages many legitimate business owners to remain in the underground. The alternative can mean months or years of delays and costly legal assistance, if such legal help can be obtained at all. . . . Hampered by rules, costly permits and licenses, hundreds of thousands of hard working, enterprising Mexicans opt to pay bribes to bypass delays and heavy-handed governmental restrictions.[49]

As a consequence, billions of dollars in tax revenue have been lost. Most significantly, however, underground entrepreneurs are prevented from expanding their operations because they must avoid public scrutiny and legal recourse. Others are dissuaded from entrepreneurship altogether, either by the pernicious regulatory environment to which legitimate business is subjected or because they are hesitant to entertain the bribery solicitations of public officials. The Mexican experience is replicated in other Latin American countries, where, Bela Balassa argues, potential economic activity is similarly suppressed:

> Excessive regulations thus costs Latin American economies dearly. Overregulation requires a large government administrative apparatus,

imposes a burden on private business in the formal sector, provides
incentives but also some disincentives to the informal sector, and contributes to a misallocation of resources. It also hampers rapid and flex-
ible response to market conditions.[50]

The expressed sentiments of CDC-Mexico executives and entrepreneurs with respect to the government's regulatory role in affecting
their business activity illustrates the cited problems. One executive
complains: "The government hasn't done anything positive. There
are lots of regulations—vendors are very unhappy. Nobody is creating good outputs as a result of the enormous amount of regulations
in force. The government puts unique regulations in place without
consulting experts or the vendors."

Furthermore, government regulations and practices are particularly burdensome upon the private firms with which it does business.
As the state is a major consumer in Mexico, this effect is strong and
pervasive, serving to depress national productivity. A CDC executive
comments on doing business with the government: "You have to
approach government in the traditional way, with lots of personal
contacts and lots of daily contact. The government expects you to pay
the costs for benchmarking, demonstrations, etc. . . . The government
asks for many, many things." Another CDC-Mexico executive complains: "There is no bribery but lots of favors. We might take a
[government employee] to the show, paying for tickets and expenses
and try to write these expenses into the contract. We also give presents."

In a positive vein, the same executives see a very recent shift in
government attitudes and regulations:

> We are now beginning a dialogue with government agencies to
> create something new because regulatory compliance is taking such a
> long time and is creating more government expenses. . . . [With respect
> to contract protocol], government now recognizes that their practices
> work against them, because all the expenses that they oblige companies
> to incur are charged to the government. I think that austerity is mag-
> nificent. The government can't continue being a developer of the coun-
> try. It has to become a promoter.

In order to be conducive to the expansion of private business
initiative and investment, the Mexican regulatory environment must
be streamlined and reoriented to the goal of better securing property
rights, which, Balassa states, should be "exclusive, partitionable, di-

visible, and perceived to be permanent."[51] Balassa believes that modernizing the legal and political institutions would accomplish these objectives:

> The process of registration and licensing should be simplified and speeded up. Contractual rights should be strengthened and an efficient tort system established. There is further need for a modern bankruptcy system that facilitates the transfer of assets from bankrupt companies to more efficient users.
>
> At the same time, rules and regulations have to be formulated and applied generally so as to curtail drastically the scope for discretionary decision making. Stability in the regulations should be ensured, and any new regulations should have to pass a cost-benefit test.[52]

Mexico has recently been taking steps, against much internal resistance, to transform their institutions in conformity with securing the aforementioned property rights. In 1982, reforms were first initiated under former President Miguel de la Madrid's "aperatura" (opening) policy and have been expanded and intensified by his successor, President Carlos Salinas de Gortari. Tax rates have been lowered, from 42 percent to 36 percent for corporations, and from 15 percent to 12 percent for lower-middle-income individuals.[53] To date, approximately 700 out of 1,000 government-owned corporations have either been allowed to go out of business or have been privatized. Although most of these 700 businesses were small, President Salinas has included some of the larger state-controlled corporations in the privatization scheme while offering foreign investors equity participation. Authorized foreign investment averaged only $2.2 billion during the Madrid administration, and Salinas has been eager to attract more, planning for twice as much ($4.5 billion) by the mid-1990s.[54] With respect to fdi, Madrid's aperatura reforms had little effect on investor confidence, for they did not address the 1973 Foreign Investment Law. Instead, foreign investors at the time were assured that government would "look away," allowing their particular (but illegal) investment to proceed unhindered. Not surprisingly, this approach did not inspire investor confidence.

Changing course, Salinas liberalized the foreign investment regulations in May 1989 to "allow foreign participation in some previously closed sectors, such as airlines, and provide for automatic approval of projects of as much as $100 million in industries not reserved for public or national companies."[55] Still, foreign investors have remained skeptical and are awaiting full implementation of the promised reforms, for the 1989 regulations do not actually repeal the 1973 law but instead rely on circuitous and creative mechanisms "such as special 20-year trusts [to] . . . allow foreigners to enter some once closed industries."[56] Aware of continued investor skepticism, Salinas stepped up the pace, and in August 1989 announced plans to reduce Mexico's 58 percent stake in Mexicana de Aviación over the next three years, while allowing for foreign majority ownership.[57] To further convince doubters, Salinas has accepted foreign projects in the previously exclusive telecommunications industry. Most notably, in 1989 Salinas authorized privatization of Teléfonos de México [Telmex], the government's notoriously inefficient telephone monopoly,[58] and in December 1990 a consortium of Mexican investors, along with the Southwestern Bell Corporation and France Telecom, bought a controlling interest in Telmex for $1.76 billion.[59] Also in 1990, the Mexican government announced a bank privatization program with plans to privatize 18 small, medium, and large banks that were nationalized in 1982. The privatizations are intended for completion in 1993, and foreign investment will be allowed to reach up to 30 percent of a bank's capital.[60]

With respect to indigenously owned business, government has sought to incite international competitiveness; the maximum tariff on imports has been lowered to 20 percent from a 1983 high of 100 percent as Mexico finally became a signatory to GATT.[61] And on a North American basis, a free trade agreement with the United States and Canada would promise to phase out these tariffs altogether in many sectors. Furthermore, government cutbacks in spending and new investment, along with other economic reforms, have helped to sustain a more stable peso and a less inflationary economy during 1989–1991.[62] These measures have drawn praise from the international financial community, which is eager to see Mexico on a sound financial footing and able to repay its roughly $80 billion in foreign loans.[63]

Greater and more extensive reforms are necessary. Although commitments by Salinas have been made, the intellectual property rights of foreign businesses are still not well protected in Mexico, and lowered import tariffs are still far above the roughly 4 percent average of industrialized nations.[64] Perhaps the most difficult to reform will be the sea of red tape and corruption attached to government bureaucracy. Indeed, Alejandro Junco has noted the warning that "it's faster and easier to sign free-trade agreements externally than it is to develop a competitive market system internally."[65] In this respect, Salinas has surprised most onlookers with his courage, dramatically demonstrated by his arrest of the previously "untouchable" PEMEX union boss "La Quina," the Jimmy Hoffa of Mexican labor. Whether other interests will also collapse from Salinas's attempts to root out corruption is still uncertain.

For Salinas to effect changes, he will need the allegiance of the Mexican people, who have suffered a 50 percent drop in real purchasing power between 1982 and 1989.[66] In order to gain their support, political institutions must be more receptive to popular will. In this respect, freer elections that remove the corrupt stranglehold of the ruling Institutional Revolutionary Party (PRI) on public office will be critical. Salinas has taken unprecedented action in countenancing opposition-party victories in certain elections, which may be construed as his acknowledgement that pluralistic democracy may be a necessary accomplice to sustained market-oriented development. Nonetheless, the PRI apparatus is not well controlled by Salinas and may prove to be resilient to his attempted reform efforts.

In conclusion, the effort to expand indigenous entrepreneurship in Mexico and Canada necessitates the implementation of market-oriented institutional arrangements, the relaxation of import substitution policies, and the reform of other discriminatory policies that depress the potential for long-term growth and development.

Conclusion

The analysis of Control Data Corporation's activities in Mexico and Canada provides strong support for the modernization perspective, demonstrating the means by which MNC subsidiaries may diffuse their advanced technological capabilities and managerial skills to benefit indigenous enterprise. Furthermore, Control Data's record provides evidence that the MNC's stimulation of entrepreneurship may be manifest without significant accompanying preemption or displacement of other indigenous entrepreneurship, contradicting the charges of dependency theorists.

Thus, the effort to expand indigenous entrepreneurship in Mexico and Canada should not be undertaken through the constraint of multinational investment. To the contrary, reforms should be more liberally conceived, with the goal of best harnessing free-market forces in mind. State programs of this design would relax import substitution policies that unevenly favor designated companies or industries while depressing competition, business incentive, and the potential for long term growth and development.

According to modernization theory, the majority share of responsibility for continued stagnation is charged to the policies and practices of the underdeveloped state; therefore, the revision of institutional arrangements along the advised lines is expected to result in a more productive economy, where greater and new investment is encouraged and privately directed toward production in areas where indigenous business possesses a comparative advantage.

In the reformed polities, superior technology and advanced managerial practices are expected to accelerate in their diffusion to indigenous parties, and, significantly, this transfer of knowledge will be activated, more productively utilized, and sustained by easier taxes, regulations, and the securing of other property rights. In such an environment, the discriminatory incentives of misguided industrial policies are replaced by freer, market-oriented incentives, expected to prove more adept than government in efficiently directing investment. The result will be increasing levels of successful indigenous entrepreneurship.

In such a context, the MNC subsidiary will serve as a critical element in development's advance guard, particularly in those countries where indigenous industrial entrepreneurship is most lacking. Subsequently, as indigenous entrepreneurship learns and expands alongside fdi, domestic self-reliance will proportionately increase, laying the groundwork for more robust and sustained development.

Notes

Introduction

1. This rigor is too infrequently attempted when evaluating the impact of multinational investment. For example, Thomas J. Biersteker comments that most research has been conducted "with little concern for addressing systematically the central propositions of alternative perspectives." See Biersteker, *Distortion or Development?: Contending Perspectives on the Multinational Corporation* (Cambridge, Mass.: MIT Press, 1978), ii.

Chapter 1

1. The world population was 4.82 billion in 1985. See *The World in Figures* (London: Economist Publications, 1985), 8.

2. LDCs are alternatively classified as "developing," "underdeveloped," or "poor."

3. Compare the $50 per capita income in Chad to the $16,100 in the United Arab Emirates. See *The World in Figures,* 13.

4. Ibid.

5. Montek S. Ahluwalia, "Income Inequality: Some Dimensions of the Problem," in Hollis Chenery, et al., *Redistribution with Growth* (London: Oxford University Press, 1974), 7. The Gini coefficient is another commonly utilized measure of income inequality, possessing a value of zero in cases of complete equality and attaining a value of 1 in cases where one individual possesses all the wealth. In 1978, for example, 96 LDCs had a population-weighted Gini coefficient of 0.54 as compared to a 0.13 coefficient for 20 developed countries. See Ian M. D. Little, *Economic Development: Theory, Policy, and International Relations* (New York: Basic Books, 1982), 271.

6. William M. Murdoch, *The Poverty of Nations: The Political Economy of Hunger and Population* (Baltimore: Johns Hopkins University Press, 1980), 10.

128

7. Ibid.

8. See, for example, J. de Hoogh, et al., "Food for a Growing World Population," *European Review of Agricultural Economics* 3 (1977): 455–499.

9. Little, *Economic Development,* 212.

10. William J. Dixon, "Progress in Provision of Basic Human Needs: Latin America, 1960–1980," *Journal of Developing Areas* (January 1987): 129–140, citing data from World Bank, *World Development Report 1982* (New York: Oxford University Press, 1982). Three component indicators—infant mortality, life expectancy at age one, and literacy—make up the PQLI.

11. Ibid., 133.

12. Richard Easterlin, "Does Economic Growth Improve the Human Lot?" in David Paul and Melvin Reeder, eds., *Nations and Households in Economic Growth: Essays in Honor of Moses Abramowitz* (New York: Academic Press, 1974).

13. Little, *Economic Development,* 271.

14. Ibid., 277.

15. Ibid., 279.

16. Note that the record for many LDCs in the 1980s has shown diminished growth both in absolute terms and with respect to developed countries. For example, Africa's per capita income is below what it was in 1980, indicating that real growth for the continent was overwhelmed by population growth. See Roger Thurow, "Africa's Poorest Nations Press Debt Relief," *Wall Street Journal* (September 21, 1988): A22.

17. Some economists have forwarded minimalist, pareto-efficient solutions for effecting distributive justice, although this may be seen as a venture into the political domain. See Robert Gilpin, *U.S. Power and the Multinational Corporation: The Political Economy of Foreign Direct Investment* (New York: Basic Books, 1975), 35. Pareto efficiency exists if no transaction is available which would make at least one person better off and no one else worse off. See James E. Alt and K. Alec Chrystal, *Political Economics* (Los Angeles: University of California Press, 1983), 183.

18. Supply-side advocate Jude Wanniski advances a similar argument in calling for lower marginal tax rates. See Wanniski, *The Way the World Works: How Economies Fail—and Succeed* (New York: Basic Books, 1978).

19. Gilpin, *U.S. Power and the Multinational Corporation,* 34–35.

20. However, with respect to government's international role, Malthus's support of the Corn Laws stands in great contrast to Ricardo's call for free trade in goods for which the nation possesses a comparative advantage in production. See, for example, Jacob Oser, *The Evolution of Economic Thought* (New York: Harcourt, Brace and World, 1963), 48–84.

21. David Bright Singh, *Economics of Development* (New York: Asia Publishing, 1966), 37, citing Adam Smith's *Wealth of Nations*.

22. Oser, *The Evolution of Economic Thought,* 48–84. Smith prophesied decay due to increasing competition and constant returns to capital; Ricardo, due to diminishing marginal returns; and Malthus, due to the inability of food production to keep pace with population growth.

23. Adam Smith, *An Inquiry Into the Nature and Causes of the Wealth of Nations,* Edwin Cannan, ed. (New York: Random House, 1937), Book 1, Chapter 8.

24. David Ricardo, *Works and Correspondence,* Piero Sraffa, ed. (Cambridge: Cambridge University Press, 1951), Volume 1, 392.

25. The neoclassical school developed out of the marginalist school's synthesis with the classical school, first accomplished by Alfred Marshall. Basically, the classical school had emphasized the cost of production and supplies as determining price while the marginalist school had emphasized demand. Price determination, in Marshall's neoclassical synthesis, was based on the economic Law of Supply and Demand.

26. John D. Wisman, "The Methodology of W. Arthur Lewis's Development Economics," *World Development* 14, no. 2 (1986): 169.

27. Although growth and rising inequality are frequently linked (e.g., Brazil 1960–1970 and Mexico 1963–1968), a comprehensive survey of the literature "suggests that there is little firm empirical basis for the views that higher rates of growth inevitably generate greater inequality." See Ahluwalia, "Income Inequality," 13.

28. J. Samuel Valenzuela and Arturo Valenzuela, "Modernization and Dependency: Alternative Perspectives in the Study of Latin American Underdevelopment," in Heraldo Munoz, ed. *From Dependency to Development* (Boulder, Colo.: Westview, 1981), 21.

29. Seymour M. Lipset, "Values, Education, and Entrepreneurship," in Lipset and Aldo Solari, eds. *Elites in Latin America* (New York: Oxford University Press, 1963), 30. Some of the studies cited include T. C. Cochran, "Cultural Factors in Economic Growth," *Journal of Economic History* 20 (1974); Tomás R. Fillol, *Social Factors*

in Economic Development: The Argentine Case (Cambridge, Mass.:
MIT Press, 1961); B. J. Siegel, "Social Structures and Economic
Change in Brazil," in Simon Kuznets, et. al., *Economic Growth: Brazil, India, Japan* (Durham, N.C.: Duke University Press, 1955); and
W. P. Straasman, "The Industrialist," in John J. Johnson, ed., *Continuity and Change in Latin America* (Stanford: Stanford University
Press, 1964).

30. Gary Gereffi, *The Pharmaceutical Industry and Dependency
in the Third World* (Princeton, N.J.: Princeton University Press,
1985), 4. Gereffi cites the best-known formulations of the polar social
categories of tradition and modernity. See, for example, Sir Henry
Maine's distinction between status- and contract-based societies in
his *Ancient Law: its Connection with the Early history of Society and
Its Relation to Modern Ideas* (New York: Dutton, 1861). Gereffi also
cites works by Ferdinand Toennies (1887), Emile Durkheim (1893),
Herbert Spencer (1850), Karl Marx (1867), and Max Weber (1922).

31. Gereffi, *The Pharmaceutical Industry*, 4. For example, from
economics (Rostow, 1960; Hoselitz, 1960), political science (Almond
and Coleman, 1960), sociology (Lerner, 1958; Inkeles, 1969), psychology (McClelland, 1961; Hagen, 1962), and history (Black, 1966).

32. Valenzuela and Valenzuela, "Modernization and Dependency," 22, citing Lipset, "Values, Education, and Entrepreneurship," 3–60.

33. George S. Masannat, "Persistence and Transformation of
Traditional Societies," *Journal of Developing Societies* 3 (1987): 114.

34. R. Scott, "Political Elites," in Lipset and Solari, eds., *Elites
in Latin America,* 133.

35. Douglass C. North and Robert Paul Thomas, *The Rise of the
Western World: A New Economic History* (Cambridge: Cambridge
University Press, 1973), 1.

36. North, "Beyond the New Economic History," *Journal of Economic History* 34 (March 1974): 2.

37. In addition, commerce was stifled in both countries from
excessive and unevenly applied regulations and high taxation, as representative bodies relinquished authority to the Crown in exchange
for order and stability. See North and Thomas, *The Rise of the Western World,* 127.

38. North and Thomas, *The Rise of the Western World,* 157.

39. Ibid.

40. Gereffi, *The Pharmaceutical Industry,* 7.

41. Modernization theory has served as an instrument of state

promotion for the United States. For example, Bert Hoselitz's *Socio-logical Aspects of Economic Growth* (Glencoe, Ill.: Free Press, 1960) was translated into 25 languages by the U.S. Department of State. Myron Weiner's *Modernization: The Dynamics of Growth* (New York: Basic Books, 1966) is a collection of essays by modernization writers which were first prepared for the "Voice of America" radio broadcasting organization.

42. See, for example, Joseph R. Gusfield, "Tradition and Modernity: Misplaced Polarities in the Study of Social Change," *American Journal of Sociology* 72 (1967): 351–362.

43. Gilpin, *The Political Economy of International Relations* (Princeton, N.J.: Princeton University Press, 1987), 274.

44. Other early structuralist writers include Paul Rosenstein Rodan, Ragnar Nurkse, Hans Singer, and Gunnar Myrdal.

45. Gilpin, *The Political Economy of International Relations,* 274–275.

46. The existence of deteriorating terms of trade for LDCs as a secular trend is widely disputed. See Gilpin, *The Political Economy of International Relations,* 299. Gilpin also claims that the argument may be beyond resolution (281).

47. High costs were often the result of inefficiencies induced by non-competitiveness and by low scale-economies due to being limited to a typically small LDC market.

48. Osvaldo Sunkel, "Big Business and Dependencia," *Foreign Affairs* 52 (April 1972): 522.

49. Andre Gunder Frank, *Capitalism and Underdevelopment in Latin America: Historical Studies of Chile and Brazil* (New York: Monthly Review Press, 1969), xi.

50. Theotonio Dos Santos, "The Structures of Dependency," in K. T. Fann and Donald C. Hodges, eds., *Readings in U.S. Imperialism* (Boston: P. Sargent, 1971), 234.

51. James H. Weaver and Marguerite Berger, "The Marxist Critique of Dependency Theory," in Charles K. Wilber, ed., *The Political Economy of Development and Underdevelopment,* 3d ed. (New York: Random House, 1984), 55.

52. Karl Marx and Fredrick Engels, *The Communist Manifesto* (London: Pelican, 1967), 84.

53. Geoffrey Kay, *Development and Underdevelopment* (New York: Macmillan, 1975), 4.

54. Among those prominent writers who advocate socialist revolution are Andre Gunder Frank, Theotonio Dos Santos, Fernando

H. Cardoso and Enzo Faletto. Socialist revolution in the early stages of capitalist development was successfully promoted by Lenin with the Bolshevik Revolution, a reason for the frequent classification of dependency theory as neo-Marxist.

55. The position often associated with Andre Gunder Frank.

56. The position associated with Fernando Cardoso and Enzo Faletto. See Cardoso and Faletto, *Dependency and Development in Latin America,* Marjory M. Urquidi, trans. (Berkeley: University of California Press, 1979).

57. Gilpin, *The Political Economy of International Relations,* 296.

58. Paul Leo Eckbo, *The Future of World Oil* (Cambridge, Mass.: Ballinger, 1976).

59. Gilpin, *The Political Economy of International Relations,* 299.

60. Chung-in Moon, "Complex Interdependence and Transnational Lobbying: South Korea in the United States," *International Studies Quarterly* 32 (1988): 68. A growing number of scholars have raised the possibility that asymmetrical power relations do not always impose inescapable constraints on the weak. For example, see Charles F. Doran, "Structuring the Concept of Dependency Reversal," in Doran, George Modelski, and Cal Clark, eds., *North/South Relations: Studies of Dependency Reversal* (New York: Praeger, 1983), 1–27. See also William Zartman, *The Policies of Trade Negotiation Between Africa and the EEC: The Weak Confronts the Strong* (Princeton, N.J.: Princeton University Press, 1971).

61. Gereffi, *The Pharmaceutical Industry,* 31.

62. Robert O. Keohane and Joseph S. Nye, Jr., "Power and Interdependence Revisited," *International Organization* 4 (Autumn 1987): 726.

63. Larry Diamond, "Strategies for Democratization," *Washington Quarterly* 12 (Winter 1989): 150.

64. Jonathan Lemco, "Economic and Political Development in Modernizing States," *Journal of Developing Societies* 4 (1988): 14.

65. Cardoso is quoted in Albert Berry, "Poverty and Inequality in Latin America," *Latin American Research Review* 22 (1987): 207.

66. Ibid.

67. See Biersteker, "Critical Reflections on Post-Positivism in International Relations," *International Studies Quarterly* 33 (1989): 264.

68. Ibid., 265–266.

69. See Biersteker, *Distortion or Development?* See also Christopher Chase-Dunne, "Inequality, Structural Mobility, and Dependency Reversal in the Capitalist World Economy," 73–95, and Volker Bornschier, "Dependent Reproduction in the World System," 97–116, in Doran, Modelski, and Clark, eds., *North/South Relations.*

70. Doran, "Structuring the Concept of Dependency Reversal," in Doran, Modelski, and Clark, eds., *North/South Relations,* 1.

71. Capitalist O.E.C.D. countries tend to demonstrate superior economic growth relative to the leading communist nations, whereas communist nations generally fare better with respect to income equality.

72. Doran, Modelski, and Clark, "Introduction," in Doran, Modelski, and Clark, eds., *North-South Relations,* xiv, discussing Robert A. Packenham, "The Dependency Perspective and Analytic Dependency," in *North-South Relations,* 29–47.

73. Ibid., xv, discussing Packenham, "The Dependency Perspective and Analytic Dependency."

74. Martin Fransman, "Conceptualizing Technical Change in the Third World in the 1980s: An Interpretive Survey," *Journal of Development Studies* 21 (July 1985): 607–608.

75. Bill Warren, *Imperialism: Pioneer of Capitalism* (London: NLB, 1980), 161, citing the position of "mainstream" dependency writers (e.g., Cardoso, Falletto, Evans, etc.).

76. Peter B. Evans expresses this idea. See, for example, Evans, "State Capital and the Transformation of Dependence: The Brazilian Computer Case," *World Development* 14, no. 7 (1986): 791–808.

Chapter 2

1. Under Cole's stewardship, the center (founded in 1948 and disbanded ten years later) served to elevate the status of entrepreneurship as a field of important scholarly inquiry and succeeded to attract scholars from a variety of disciplines (e.g., Joseph Schumpeter, Thomas Cochran, Alexander Gershenkron).

2. Arthur H. Cole, "An Approach to the Study of Entrepreneurship," in Hugh G. J. Aitken, ed., *Explorations in Enterprise* (Cambridge, Mass.: Harvard University Press, 1965), 32.

3. Mark Casson, *The Entrepreneur: An Economic Theory* (Totowa, N.J.: Barnes and Noble, 1982), 9.

4. Peter Kilby, "The Role of Alien Entrepreneurs in Economic

Development: An Entrepreneurial Problem," *American Economic Review* 73, no. 2 (1983): 107.

5. Kilby, "Hunting the Heffalump," in Kilby, ed., *Entrepreneurship and Economic Development* (New York: Free Press, 1971), 3.

6. Jean-Baptiste Say, *Catechism of Political Economy* (London, 1816), 28–29.

7. Jean-Baptiste Say, *A Treatise on Political Economy* (London, 1821), Volume I, 104. The first French edition of Say's book appeared in 1803. Joseph A. Schumpeter, "Economic Theory and Entrepreneurial History," in Aitken, ed., *Explorations in Enterprise,* 46, suggests that Say was influenced by Cantillon, the French economist who first introduced the term "entrepreneur" to describe the individual who "buys means of production at certain prices in order to combine them into a product that he is going to sell at prices that are uncertain at the moment at which he commits himself to his costs."

8. Schumpeter, *The Theory of Economic Development* (Cambridge, Mass.: Harvard University Press, 1934), reprinted as "The Fundamental Phenomenon of Economic Development," in Kilby, ed., *Entrepreneurship and Economic Development,* 45–46.

9. Ibid.

10. Schumpeter, "The Fundamental Phenomenon of Economic Development," in Kilby, ed., *Entrepreneurship and Economic Development,* 57.

11. Calvin E. Kent, Donald L. Sexton, Karl H. Vesper, eds., *Encyclopedia of Entrepreneurship* (Englewood Cliffs, N.J.: Prentice-Hall, 1982), 40. The significance of the managerial function of the entrepreneur can be punctuated by the following Chinese proverb: "To open a business very easy. To keep it open, very difficult." To illustrate, despite a great number of business startups in the United States, only one-third remain in business four years. See Kent, Sexton, and Vesper, eds., *Encyclopedia of Entrepreneurship,* 194.

12. Benjamin Higgins, *Economic Development* rev. ed. (New York: Norton, 1968).

13. W. Arthur Lewis, *The Theory of Economic Growth* (London: Allen and Unwin, 1955), 182. A similar prominence is given to LDC entrepreneurship in Walt W. Rostow, *The Stages of Economic Growth: A Non-Communist Manifesto* (Cambridge: Cambridge University Press, 1967), 8.

14. A. O. Hirschman, *The Strategy of Economic Development* (New Haven, Conn.: Yale University Press, 1958), 35.

15. World Bank presidential address by Robert S. McNamara, 29 September 1969.

16. Dwirjendra Tripathi, "Occupational Mobility and Industrial Entrepreneurship in India: A Historical Analysis," *Developing Economies* 19 (March 1981): 53, citing Cole, *Business Enterprise in Its Social Setting* (Cambridge, Mass.: Harvard University Press, 1959), 28; United Nations, Department of Economic and Social Affairs, *Processes and Problems of Industrialization in Underdeveloped Countries* (New York: United Nations, 1955), 30–38; Hirschman, *The Strategy of Economic Development,* 1.

17. Robert B. Buchele, "The Development of Small Industrial Entrepreneurs as a Tool of Economic Growth," (Honolulu, Hawaii: Technology and Development Institute—East/West Center, Working Paper Series No. 31, October 1972), 11, citing the trend noted by Kilby, "Preface," 5; Wayne Nafziger, "Indian Entrepreneurship: A Survey," 287; and Gustav F. Papanek, "The Development of Entrepreneurship," 317–318; all in Kilby, ed., *Entrepreneurship and Economic Development.*

18. E. O. Akeredolu-Ale, "Environmental, Organizational, and Group Factors in the Evolution of Private Indigenous Entrepreneurship in Nigeria," *Nigerian Journal of Economic and Social Studies,* 14 (July 1972): 237–256.

19. Hirschman, *The Strategy of Economic Development,* 35.

20. Robert B. Sutcliffe, *Industry and Underdevelopment* (London: Addison Wesley, 1971), Chapter 4, Section 4.7.

21. Charles F. Doran, "Structuring the Concept of Dependency Reversal," in Doran, George Modelski, and Cal Clark, eds., *North/ South Relations: Studies of Dependency Reversal* (New York: Praeger, 1983), 1.

22. See Max Weber, *The Protestant Ethic and the Spirit of Capitalism,* Talcott Parsons, trans. (London: Allen and Unwin, 1930).

23. David A. McClelland, *The Achieving Society* (Princeton: Van Nostrand, 1961), 341–356.

24. Ibid., 2.

25. For example, Bert Hoselitz claimed that "few will be able to deny the power of McClelland's case and none will be able to adduce convincing evidence to refute the assertion that *n* Achievement is one of the principal factors in economic growth." See Hoselitz, book review of McClelland's *The Achieving Society* in *American Journal of Sociology* 68 (July 1962): 130.

26. Kilby, "Hunting the Heffalump," 19.

27. McClelland, *The Achieving Society,* 102.

28. Sayre P. Schatz, "*n* Achievement and Economic Growth: A Critical Appraisal," in Kilby, ed., *Entrepreneurship and Economic Growth,* 185–186.

29. McClelland, "Entrepreneurship and Achievement Motivation," in P. Lengyel, ed., *Approaches to the Science of Socioeconomic Development* (Paris: UNESCO, 1971).

30. Kilby, "Hunting the Heffalump," 21.

31. Everett E. Hagen, "How Economic Growth Begins: A Theory of Social Change," *Journal of Social Issues* (January 1963): 33.

32. William J. Fleming, "The Cultural Determinants of Entrepreneurship and Economic Development: A Case Study of Mendoza Province, Argentina, 1861–1914," *Journal of Economic History* 39 (March 1979): 214.

33. Ibid., 215.

34. Kent, Sexton, and Vesper, eds., *Encyclopedia of Entrepreneurship,* 76, citing Erik Dahmien, *Entrepreneurial Activity and the Development of Swedish Industry, 1919–1939* (Homewood, Ill.: Irwin, 1970).

35. Benjamin Higgins, *Economic Development,* rev. ed. (New York: Norton, 1968), 245–246, summarizing unpublished seminar paper, William Long, 253–257.

36. Kilby, "Hunting the Heffalump," 1.

37. Sidney M. Greenfield and Arnold Strickon, eds., *Entrepreneurship and Social Change* (New York: University Press of America, 1986), 11, summarizing William P. Glade, "Approaches to a Theory of Entrepreneurial Formation," *Explorations in Entrepreneurial History* 2d series 4 (1967): 245–259.

38. Hoselitz, *Sociological Aspects of Economic Growth* (Glencoe, Ill.: Free Press, 1960), 155.

39. Harvey Liebenstein, *General X-Efficiency Theory and Economic Development* (New York: Oxford University Press, 1978), 53.

40. Wayne G. Broehl, Jr., "Entrepreneurship in the Less Developed World," in Kent, Sexton, and Vesper, eds., *Encyclopedia of Entrepreneurship,* 266, citing Harvey Liebenstein *Beyond Economic Man: A New Foundation for Microeconomics* (Cambridge, Mass.: Harvard University Press, 1976).

41. Ibid., citing Harvey Liebenstein, "Entrepreneurship and Development," *American Economic Review Papers and Proceedings* (May 1968), 58.

42. Liebenstein, *General X-Efficiency,* 54.

43. Broehl, "Entrepreneurship in the Less Developed World," in Kent, Sexton, and Vesper, eds., *Encyclopedia of Entrepreneurship*, 266, citing Israel M. Kirzner, *Competition and Entrepreneurship* (Chicago: University of Chicago Press, 1973).

44. Kirzner, *Discovery and the Capitalist Process* (Chicago: University of Chicago Press, 1985), 91. Some of the associated entrepreneurial gains to which Kirzner refers are as follow: "[1] a free and open economy that permits equal access to entrepreneurial opportunities, [2] guarantees of ownership in property legally acquired, and [3] stability of institutional practices that establish point 1 and 2." See also R. F. Hebert and A. N. Link, *The Entrepreneur: Mainstream Views and Radical Critiques* (New York: Praeger, 1982), 11.

Chapter 3

1. They were aided in their expansion with capital from strong economic growth and unprecedented levels of foreign lending. See Bela Balassa, et al., *Toward Renewed Economic Growth in Latin America* (Washington, D.C.: Institute for International Economics, 1986), 125.

2. In this respect, Korea and Taiwan may be cited as notable exceptions, not lacking in entrepreneurship, while having experienced strong economic growth with relatively equitable distribution. See David Morawetz, *25 Years of Economic Development: 1950–1975* (Baltimore: Johns Hopkins University Press, 1977), 69.

3. Based on total value in 1985, *The World in Figures* (London: Economist Publications, 1985), 9.

4. Elias H. Tuma, "Institutionalized Obstacles to Development: the Case of Egypt," *World Development* 16, no. 10 (1988): 1191.

5. Ibid.

6. Peter B. Evans, *Dependent Development: The Alliance of Multinational, State, and Local Capital in Brazil* (Princeton, N.J.: Princeton University Press, 1979), 9.

7. Ibid., 12.

8. Ibid., 27.

9. Michael Shafer, "Capturing the Mineral Multinationals: Advantage or Disadvantage?" in Theodore H. Moran, ed., *Multinational Corporations: The Political Economy of Foreign Direct Investment* (Lexington, Mass.: Heath, 1985), 24–53.

10. Ibid.

11. Ibid., 48.

12. Wolfgang G. Friedmann and George Kalmanoff, *Joint International Business Ventures* (New York: Columbia University Press, 1961), 4.

13. Harvard University, *Management Problems and Opportunities for Management Training in Central America,* 60, cited by Lawrence G. Franko, Michael Dixon, and Carlos Arturo Marulanda R., *Entrepreneurship and Industrialization in Latin America, Studies in Latin-American Business, No. 4* (Austin: Bureau of Business Research, University of Texas, 1966), 8.

14. See, for example, Raymond Vernon, *Sovereignty at Bay: The Multinational Spread of U.S. Enterprises* (New York: Basic Books, 1971); Theodore H. Moran, *Multinational Corporations and the Politics of Dependence: Copper in Chile* (Princeton, N.J.: Princeton University Press, 1974); David N. Smith and Louis T. Wells, Jr., *Negotiating Third World Mineral Agreements* (Cambridge, Mass.: Ballinger, 1975).

15. Moran, "Multinational Corporations and the Developing Countries," in Moran, *Multinational Corporations: The Political Economy of Foreign Direct Investment,* 6.

16. Ibid.

17. Gary Gereffi, "The Renegotiation of Dependency and the Limits of State Autonomy in Mexico (1975–1980)" in Moran, *Multinational Corporations,* 83.

18. George Philip, "The Limitations of Bargaining Theory: A Case Study of the International Petroleum Company in Peru," *World Development* 4 (March 1976): 231.

19. Ibid., 232.

20. Stephen J. Kobrin, "Testing the Bargaining Hypothesis in the Manufacturing Sector in Developing Countries," *International Organization* 41 (Autumn 1987): 610.

21. Ibid., 612.

22. Ibid.

23. Moran, "International Political Risk Assessment, Corporate Planning, and Strategies to Offset Political Risk," in Moran, *Multinational Corporations: The Political Economy of Foreign Direct Investment,* 113. Relative to MNC strategies, Moran cites David G. Bradley, "Managing Against Expropriation," *Harvard Business Review* (July-August 1977). See also Nathan Fagre and Louis T. Wells, Jr., "Bargaining Power of Multinational and Host Governments," *Journal of International Business Studies* (Fall 1982).

24. Moran, "International Political Risk Assessment, Corporate

Planning, and Strategies to Offset Political Risk," in Moran, *Multinational Corporations: The Political Economy of Foreign Direct Investment*, 113.

25. Ibid., 115, citing Stephen J. Kobrin, "The Forced Divestment of Foreign Enterprise in the LDCs," *International Organization* 34 (Winter 1980): 65–88.

26. Gary Gereffi, "The Renegotiation of Dependency and the Limits of State Autonomy in Mexico (1975–1982)," in Moran, *Multinational Corporations: The Political Economy of Foreign Direct Investment*, 100.

27. Alfred C. Stepan, *The State and Society: Peru in Comparative Perspective* (Princeton, N.J.: Princeton University Press, 1978), 235.

28. See Joseph M. Grieco, "Between Dependency and Autonomy: India's Experience with the International Computer Industry," *International Organization* 36 (Summer 1982), 609–632.

29. IBM installed almost three-quarters of all computer systems between 1967 and 1972.

30. See Emanuel Adler, "Ideological 'Guerrillas' and the Quest for Technological Autonomy: Brazil's Domestic Computer Industry," *International Organization* 40 (Summer 1986), 673–705.

31. Evans, "State, Capital, and the Transformation of Dependence: The Brazilian Computer Case," *World Development* 14, no. 7 (1986): 791.

32. Adler, "State Institutions, Ideology, and Autonomous Technological Development: Computers and Nuclear Energy in Argentina and Brazil," *Latin American Research Review* 23, no. 2 (1988): 64.

33. Joseph M. Grieco, "Between Dependency and Autonomy," in Moran, *Multinational Corporations: The Political Economy of Foreign Direct Investment*, 57.

34. Evans, "State, Capital, and the Transformation of Dependence," 791, summarizing his own argument in Evans, *Dependent Development*.

35. Ibid., 800.

36. Simon Schwartzman, "The Power of Technology," *Latin American Research Review*, 24, no. 1 (1989): 218.

37. Press note on the "New Computer Policy," Department of Electronics, Government of India, November 19, 1984.

38. "India," in Francis W. Rushing and Carole G. Brown, eds., *National Policies for Developing High Technology Industries* (Boulder, Colo.: Westview, 1986), 109.

39. Ibid.

40. Author's phone conversation with Adler, February 10, 1989. Furthermore, Adler states that the MNC also provided their former employee/entrepreneurs with special knowledge that assisted the state in pursuing a successful bargaining strategy for its dealings with multinational interests.

41. Adler, "State Institutions," 70–71.

42. FDI has indeed played a role in southeast Asian development, particularly in the higher technology industries. For example, the Korean electronics industry was dominated by fdi during the 1970s. See Larry E. Westphal, Yung W. Rhee, and Gary Pursell, "Foreign Influences on Korean Industrial Development," *Oxford Bulletin of Economic and Statistics* 41 (November 1979): 381. In the last ten years, however, this earlier dependence has been transformed. Today, the Korean electronics industry is predominantly indigenously owned and strongly competitive internationally, presumably having benefitted from its intensive prior contact with foreign investment.

43. *Investing in Developing Countries,* 5th ed., rev. (Paris: Organization for Economic Co-Operation and Development, 1982), 23.

44. Ibid., 25.

45. "Mexico Woos Foreign Investors and Rejects Them," *Economist* (February 9, 1985): 62.

46. *Employment Effects of Multinational Enterprises in Developing Countries* (Geneva: International Labour Office, 1981), 21.

47. Richard S. Newfarmer, "Multinationals and Marketplace Magic in the 1980s," in Charles K. Wilber, ed., *The Political Economy of Development and Underdevelopment,* 3d ed. (New York: Random House, 1984), 183.

48. *Investing in Developing Countries,* 25.

49. See Robert Ardrey, *The Territorial Imperative: A Personal Inquiry into the Animal Origins of Property and Nations* (New York: Atheneum, 1966).

50. *Employment Effects of Multinational Enterprises in Developing Countries,* 9.

51. Ibid.

52. Magnus Blomstrom and Hakan Persson, "Foreign Investment and Spillover Efficiency in an Underdeveloped Economy," *World Development,* 11, no. 6 (1983): 494.

53. Moran, "Multinational Corporations and the Developing

Countries: An Analytical Overview," in *Multinational Corporations: The Political Economy of Foreign Direct Investment,* 3.

54. Theotonio dos Santos, "The Structure of Dependence," *American Economic Review* 60 (1970): 235.

55. Moran, *Multinational Corporations,* 3.

56. Peter Drucker, "Multinational Corporations and Developing Countries: Myths and Realities," *Foreign Affairs* 50 (October 1974): 134.

57. Thomas J. Biersteker, *Distortion or Development?: Contending Perspectives on the Multinational Corporation* (Cambridge, Mass.: MIT Press, 1978), xii.

58. Sheldon Smith, "Entrepreneurial Agriculture and the Involution of Agricultural Dynamics in the Americas," in Sidney M. Greenfield and Arnold Strickon, eds., *Entrepreneurship and Social Change: Monographs in Economic Anthropology, No. 2* (Lanham, Md.: University Press of America, 1986), 100.

59. S. Sethi and J. Sheth, eds., *Multinational Business Operations I* (Pacific Palisades, Calif.: Goodyear Publishing Co., 1973), 171.

60. Osvaldo Sunkel, "Big Business and Dependencia: A Latin American View," *Foreign Affairs* 50 (April 1972): 527.

61. Biersteker, *Distortion or Development?,* 20.

62. *Employment Effects of Multinational Enterprises in Developing Countries,* 21.

63. Ibid., 33.

64. The Committee on the International Migration of Talent, *Modernization and the Migration of Talent* (New York: Education and World Affairs, January 1970), 42.

65. Walter Adams, *The Brain Drain* (New York: Macmillan, 1968), 1.

66. Mark Casson, *The Entrepreneur: An Economic Theory* (Totowa, N.J.: Barnes and Noble Books, 1982), 35.

67. Irving Gershenberg, "The Training and Spread of Managerial Know-How: A Comparative Analysis of Multinational and Other Firms in Kenya," *World Development* 15 (July 1987): 432.

68. Ibid.

69. *Multinational Enterprises and Social Policy* (Geneva: International Labour Office, 1973), 58.

70. Biersteker, *Distortion or Development?,* 8.

71. Richard E. Caves, "Income Distribution and Labor Relations," in Moran, *Multinational Corporations: The Political Economy*

of Foreign Direct Investment, 187, citing U.S. Tariff Commission, *Implications of Multinational Firms for World Trade and Investment and for U.S. Trade and Labor* (Washington, D.C.: U.S. Government Printing Office, 1973) and Grant L. Reuber, et al., *Private Foreign Investment in Development* (Oxford: Clarendon Press, 1973), 175–176.

72. Ibid., 188, citing K. Taira and G. Standing "Labor Market Effects of Multinational Enterprises in Latin America," *Nebraska Journal of Economic Business* 12 (Autumn 1973): 103–117.

73. Ibid., 187, citing evidence from J. H. Dunning and E. J. Morgan, "Employee Compensation in U.S. Multinationals and Indigenous Firms: An Explanatory Micro/Macro Analysis," *British Journal of Industrial Relations* 18 (July 1980): 179–201.

74. *Multinational Enterprises and Social Policy,* 57.

75. Biersteker, *Distortion or Development?,* 115.

76. Similarly, in Latin American cases it has been claimed that as much as 83 percent of MNC financing is locally obtained. See Ronald Muller, "(More) on Multinationals: Poverty is the Product," *Foreign Policy* 13 (1973–1974), 85–88. Raymond Vernon makes a similar estimation that between 75 and 80 percent of U.S. overseas financing is raised outside of the United States. See Vernon, "The Economic Consequences of U.S. Foreign Direct Investment," in Vernon, *Economic and Political Consequences of Multinational Enterprises: An Anthology* (Boston: Division of Research, Harvard Business School, 1972), 75.

77. Biersteker, *Distortion or Development?,* 115–116, citing E. O. Akeredolu-Ale, *The Underdevelopment of Indigenous Entrepreneurship in Nigeria* (Ibadan, Nigeria: Ibadan University Press, 1975), 59.

78. Ibid., 116–117, citing Akeredolu-Ale, *The Underdevelopment of Indigenous Entrepreneurship in Nigeria,* 57

79. Ibid., 100.

80. Alan Rugman, Book review of Biersteker, *Distortion or Development?, Political Science Quarterly* 94 (Winter 1980): 723-724.

81. Biersteker, *Distortion or Development?,* 118.

82. Muller, "(More) on Multinationals: Poverty is the Product," 88.

83. Biersteker, *Distortion or Development?,* 8.

84. Vernon, *Multinational Enterprises in Developing Countries: An Analysis of National Goals and Policies* (working paper) (Boston: Harvard Institute of International Development, June 1975), 2c.

85. The nonconformity of the Nigerian case to Vernon's more general finding may be exceptional due to the African context. In Latin America, the geographic area of highest MNC investment in the developing world, MNC concentration in certain industries constitutes a majority share, while market share in many other industries is substantially smaller.

86. Vernon, *The Operations of Multinational U.S. Enterprises in Developing Countries* (New York: United Nations UNCTAD TD/B/399, 1972), 22.

87. Douglas Bennett and Kenneth Sharpe, *Transnational Corporations Versus the State: The Political Economy of the Mexican Auto Industry* (Princeton, N.J.: Princeton University Press, 1983), 136.

Chapter 4

1. See Joseph M. Grieco, "Between Dependency and Development," in Theodore H. Moran, ed., *Multinational Corporations: The Political Economy of Foreign Direct Investment* (Lexington, Mass.: Heath, 1985) and Emanuel Adler, "Ideological 'Guerillas' and the Quest for Technological Autonomy: Brazil's Domestic Computer Industry," *International Organization* 40 (Summer 1986): 673–705.

2. Karl P. Sauvant, *Trade and Foreign Direct Investment in Data Services* (Boulder, Colo.: Westview, 1986), 8, citing OECD, *Interfutures: Facing the Future. Mastering the Probable and Managing the Unpredictable* (Paris: OECD, 1979).

3. Ibid., 7.

4. Peter Dicken, *Global Shift: Industrial Change in a Turbulent World* (London: Harper & Row, 1986), 317.

5. Peter B. Evans, "State, Capital, and the Transformation of Dependence: The Brazilian Computer Case," *World Development* 14 (July 1986): 804.

6. Furthermore, India's stringent restrictions on foreign investment and Brazil's licensing requirements caused them to be singled out, along with Japan in 1989, as potential subjects for U.S. retaliation in the form of quotas or punitive tariffs under the so-called "Super 301" provision of the 1988 U.S. trade law. The United States ended up taking no retaliatory actions against any of the countries, and "Super 301" has since expired. See Stephen E. Nordlinger, "U.S. Cites Three Nations Over Trade," *Baltimore Sun* (May 26, 1989): 1A.

7. Fen Osler Hampson, *Forming Economic Policy: The Case of Energy in Canada and Mexico* (New York: St. Martin's, 1986), 41.

8. Ibid., 28.

9. Ibid., 29.

10. *The World in Figures* (London: Economist Publications, 1985), 9.

11. This trade dependence on the United States is particularly amplified in the Canadian case when recognizing that the Canadian economy is highly trade oriented, with 26 percent of its GDP accounted for by exports (compared, for example, with the United States [5.4 percent] and Mexico [12.5 percent]). Trade concentration figures are calculated from GDP and export revenue data found in *The World in Figures*.

12. Dicken, *Global Shift*, 64.

13. MNC dominance in the computer industry is certainly not complete. Indigenous investors have 51 percent equity participation in several U.S. subsidiaries, and indigenous producers account for a significant amount of intermediate inputs, parts, and computer peripherals. Furthermore, indigenous producers of data services and software are a growing industrial segment in Mexico.

14. Dicken, *Global Shift*, 64.

15. John N. H. Britton and James M. Gilmour, *The Weakest Link: A Technological Perspective on Canadian Industrial Underdevelopment* (Ottawa: Science Council of Canada, 1978), 86.

16. Ibid., 99.

17. *The World in Figures*, 13.

18. Ibid., 8.

19. Ibid., 137.

20. Ranked tenth worldwide in 1985, with per capita income of U.S. $11,778. *The World in Figures*, 13.

21. *The World in Figures*, 120. Table 2 (p. 70) shows the percentage contribution of various Canadian and Mexican products to total export revenue, illustrating Canada's greater diversity.

22. George P. Muller, *Comparative World Data: A Statistical Handbook for the Social Sciences* (Baltimore: Johns Hopkins University Press, 1988) 312–314.

23. For example, the top 20 percent of individuals in Canada accumulated 40.2 percent of GNP in 1965, whereas in Mexico, the same quintile accumulated 64 percent of GNP in 1969. See Montek S. Ahluwalia, "Income Inequality: Some Dimensions of the Problem," in Hollis Chenery, et al., *Redistribution with Growth* (London: Oxford University Press, 1974), 9–10.

24. Britton and Gilmour, *The Weakest Link,* 24.

25. The dissenting view was expressed in Chapter 1 of this book.

26. Grieco, "Between Dependency and Development," in Moran, *Multinational Corporations,* 631.

27. Control Data Corporation annual report for year ended December 31, 1990. In 1988, sales were more than twice as great—$3.6 billion, making CDC the seventh largest U.S. computer industry firm at the time. See "The Largest U.S. Industrial Corporations," *Fortune* (April 24, 1989): 382. However, over the subsequent three years, CDC underwent considerable restructuring by shedding underperforming divisions in order to cut costs and restore profitability.

28. Javram Ramesh and Charles Weiss, eds., *Mobilizing Technology for World Development* (New York: Praeger, 1979), 138. Examining the mechanisms of entrepreneurship is an especially relevant endeavor for Mexico. Ramesh and Weiss state that these mechanisms are less explicitly known in LDCs.

29. In Canada, 12 entrepreneurs out of a possible thirteen were personally interviewed.

30. Yvon Gasse, "Elaborations on the Psychology of the Entrepreneur," in Calvin E. Kent, Donald L. Sexton, and Karl H. Vesper, eds., *Encyclopedia of Entrepreneurship* (Englewood Cliffs, N.J.: Prentice-Hall, 1982), 66. Low questionnaire return rates lead Gasse to emphasize the desirability of visiting the firm.

31. Data was collected from CDC-Canada (Computing Devices) and ex-employee/entrepreneurs during June/July of 1988 and from CDC-Mexico and ex-employee/entrepreneurs during November, 1988.

32. Charles K. Wilber, "Methodological Debate in Economics: Editor's Introduction," *World Development* 14 (February 1986): 144.

Chapter 5

1. Two of the enterprises were co-founded by separate pairs of former Computing Devices employees.

2. An additional entrepreneur was surveyed through written correspondence; the remaining entrepreneur, who sold his business in 1973, was not located. Alternatively, the former second in command with this business was interviewed, providing essential information regarding his former superior.

3. Three of the businesses were sold, two to Canadian firms and one to a British firm. Dipix Inc. went bankrupt in 1985. Interestingly, this "failure" was the only business that Computing Devices formally spun off from its own operations.

4. For example, crash position indicators, combustion analysis instrumentation, electronic security sensor systems.

5. The $232 million figure does not include an additional $64 million in annual revenue generated by one of the businesses. For this business, only one-half of its total of $128 million in revenue was included, for there were two founding entrepreneurs, only one of whom was a former CDC employee.

6. CDC supplies replacement parts.

7. Among these 11 franchises were the five entrepreneurs that were not interviewed. These five operations were small, recent start-ups—not contacted at CDC management's suggestion.

8. See Table 2 (p. 70).

9. They also are distributors of Unisys computers.

10. One partner generates an additional $3 million in revenue from his ownership of a number of Mexico City restaurants and night-clubs and a partnership producing plastic baggies.

11. One was educated as an industrial engineer at Stanford University; the other was formerly a tenured professor of mathematics at the National University of Mexico.

12. Average real wages in Mexico have declined by 40 percent since 1982.

13. Franchise entrepreneurs who were interviewed were located in the cities of Puebla, Tobasco, Reynosa, Chihuahua, and Mexico City.

14. On the other hand, it was noted that certain middle-tier manager/executives were reluctant to promote the franchise concept, not wanting to decrease the number of employees over whom they had direct charge.

15. A particular incident was cited as persuading a number of employees not to seek a franchise. In the incident, a franchisee was killed in an automobile accident As a self-employed contractor, he was not covered by insurance previously held when employed by CDC. As a result, his wife and children were left destitute. It is understandable that this memory has given potential franchisees pause for reflection; however, from a rational perspective, consequent rejection of a franchise is unjustified. A franchisee's first year revenues generally support a doubling of previous CDC salary; therefore, part of the differential could be invested in insurance, creating the desired family security.

16. One entrepreneur had rented out office space for a nascent computer supplies business, operating as a distributor of computer

tapes, ribbons, paper, and diskettes to local merchants. The other entrepreneur, situated in Reynosa (a U.S. border town in the state of Tamaulipas), was seeking to purchase personal computers in the United States for marked-up resale to Mexican schools and hospitals.

17. Actually, this particular franchise, located in the southern state of Tabasco, is one of the more prosperous of those surveyed, and its earnings are limited only by the entrepreneur's 80-hour work week. Unfortunately, a relative lack of educated computer professionals in Southern Mexico (and prohibitive training costs) inhibit expansion of the franchise.

18. One franchisee earns considerable revenue from computer systems consulting and another maintains a lucrative potato farm that averages $50,000 in net profits annually.

19. Calvin E. Kent, Donald A. Sexton, and Karl H. Vesper, eds., *Encyclopedia of Entrepreneurship* (Englewood Cliffs, N.J.: Prentice-Hall, 1982), 201.

20. Supporting the salience of this factor, a study of Michigan manufacturing firms by W. Hoad and P. Rosko revealed that relevant industrial experience was associated with entrepreneurial success (industrial experience was also a better predictor of success than education). See W. Hoad and P. Rosko, *Management Factors Contributing to the Success or Failure of New Small Manufacturers* (Ann Arbor: University of Michigan Press, 1964).

21. This is not a trivial finding in itself, indicating successful managers tend to make successful entrepreneurs.

22. It was stated that these regulations are rarely enforced.

23. William C. Norris, *New Frontiers for Business Leadership* (Minneapolis: Dorn, 1983), 6.

24. One individual became a self-employed consultant after being laid off when his division was phased out; another started a software engineering firm after being bored with having to be engaged in "make-work" during Computing Devices' business lull.

25. A position reporting directly to the vice president of Computing Devices.

26. In fact, it was a Canadian owned firm at the time, Mytel, which had the most recent profound influence on industry salaries, when it attempted to lure the best talent from other firms by offering 10 percent raises across the board for all technological positions.

27. Salary data was obtained from an interview with a Canadian entrepreneur in July 1988.

28. This statement assumes that higher paying government jobs were available to these individuals. The inference is corroborated through interviews. Computing Devices employees were considered to be the industry's best, and their motivation to work for Computing Devices was generally described as stemming from wanting to work with the best. Salary was never mentioned as a primary consideration.

29. Karl P. Sauvant, *Trade and Foreign Direct Investment in Data Services* (Boulder, Colo.: Westview, 1986), 87–88.

30. Ibid., 88. In fact, Brazil's weakness in software is severe, prompting the government's launching on February 27, 1991 a "Program of Industrial Competitiveness," under which Brazil ended its market reserve for software, which previously limited imports of software to those for which no "national similar" program existed. While few software imports were rejected outright—because "national similar" programs were not available—the regulatory procedures were widely criticized as time consuming, expensive, and arbitrary. See "Brazilian President Proposes Program to Modernize Industries, Investment," *Daily Executive Reporter,* no. 41 (March 1, 1991): A16.

31. Ibid., 88.

32. Mardi Wareham, *Looking Back, Reaching Forward: A History of Computing Devices Company* (in-house publication of Computing Devices Company, 6).

33. Ibid., 5.

Chapter 6

1. Debra L. Miller, "Mexico," in Francis W. Rushing and Carole G. Brown, eds., *National Policies for Developing High Technology Industries* (Boulder, Colo.: Westview, 1986), 183, in reference to Mexican Bureau of Industries, *Development Program for the Manufacturing of Electronic Computer System, Their Main Modules and Peripheral Equipment,* 2-VIII, Mexico, Federal District, 1981.

2. Ibid.

3. Ibid., 191. In concession to other manufacturers, "IBM agreed it would have no more than a 20 percent share of the local market, with the remainder of its production (over 90 percent) to be exported." Miller, "Mexico," 191.

4. Ibid., 190.

5. Ibid., 184.

6. Ibid., 185.

7. Ibid., 188, citing personal interview with Josef Warman Grieg, Director de la Industria Electronica y Coordinacion Industrial, SECOFIN, Washington, D.C., September 1985.

8. According to company executives, CDC-Mexico is allowed to gain credit for as much as 20 percent of its export requirement through its joint venture participation with the maquiladora business.

9. Miller, "Mexico," 185.

10. Ibid.

11. Most of CDC-Mexico's in-house R & D is associated with software development.

12. Miler, "Mexico," 186.

13. Ibid., 188.

14. Ibid., 184.

15. Ibid., 195.

16. Canadian rules bar foreign control of broadcasting, publishing, telecommunications, fishery, or airline companies. Robert Melnbardis and Michael T. Malloy, "Canadian Border Looks Like a Barrier to Takeover Fever," *Wall Street Journal* (September 9, 1989): C12.

17. Abraham Tarosofsky, *The Subsidization of Innovation Projects by the Government of Canada* (Ottawa: Supply and Services Canada, 1984), 27–28.

18. Ibid., 28–29.

19. Ibid., 30.

20. Donald G. McFetridge, *Technological Change in Canadian Industry* (Ottawa: Minister of Supply and Services, 1985), 29.

21. Ibid.

22. Ibid.

23. Tarasofsky, *The Subsidization of Innovation,* 63.

24. McFetridge, *Technological Change,* 31.

25. Economic Council of Canada, *The Bottom Line: Technology, Trade and Income Growth* (Ottawa: Minister of Supply and Services, 1983), 34.

26. Ibid., 37.

27. Ibid., 48.

28. Ibid.

29. "Taxing Time," *Economist,* Canadian survey issue (October 8, 1988): 10. That is, if, beginning on January 1, 1988, the salary of the average Canadian taxpayer was entirely devoted to paying off

his/her full annual tax liability to all sources, the total amount would not be paid off until July 10th—Tax Freedom Day.

30. Bruce Bartlett, "The World-Wide Tax Revolution," *Wall Street Journal* (August 29, 1989): A16. Other countries have higher tax brackets, but usually reserved for the more wealthy.

31. William Branigan, "Mexicans Await 'Brady Plan' on Debt, See it Falling Short," *Wall Street Journal* (March 28, 1989): A15.

32. Larry Rohter, "Mexico Feels Squeeze of Years of Austerity," *New York Times* (July 25, 1989): A1.

33. Dale Story, *Industry, the State, and Public Policy in Mexico* (Austin: University of Texas Press, 1986), 69.

34. Roger Cohen, "Mexican Labor Leader Wields Power to Test President Elect Salinas," *Wall Street Journal* (September 27, 1988): A1.

35. Ibid., for example.

36. Ibid., 22.

37. Ibid., 1.

38. Bela Balassa, et al., *Toward Renewed Economic Growth in Latin America* (Washington, D.C.: Institute for International Economics, 1986), 137.

39. Story, *Industry, the State, and Public Policy,* 68–69.

40. Ibid., 69.

41. Ibid.

42. Ibid., 52.

43. Peter Dicken, *Global Shift: Industrial Change in a Turbulent World* (London: Harper and Row, 1986), 151.

44. Steve Globerman, "Canada," in John H. Dunning, ed., *Multinational Enterprises, Economic Structure and International Competitiveness* (New York: Wiley, 1985), 189.

45. Dicken, *Global Shift,* 151.

46. For example, the cost of capital in Canada is approximately 3 percent higher than in the United States, increasing the risk of investment.

47. Alan Freeman, "Private Sector Gets Boost in Saskatchewan," *Wall Street Journal* (March 28, 1989): A14.

48. Marvin Alisky, "Tapping the Resources of Mexico's Underground Economy," *Wall Street Journal* (December 30, 1988): A7, citing Vera Ferrar, "The Underground Economy in Mexico" (Center for Economic Studies of the Private Sector/CEESP, August 1986).

49. Ibid.

50. Balassa, *Toward Renewed Economic Growth in Latin America,* 136.

51. Ibid.

52. Ibid.

53. David Asman, "La Perestroika Mexicana," *Wall Street Journal* (October 5, 1988): A32. The 12 percent tax rate applies at an income level of four times minimum wage.

54. Matt Moffett, "Mexico Hopes its Airline Deal Will Be Catalyst," *Wall Street Journal* (August 24, 1989): A7. Furthermore, if a North American Free Trade Agreement is implemented between the United States and Canada, one study concluded that Mexico could expect a one-time increase on investment of $25 billion, much of which might be money repatriated by Mexicans. The study, completed in February 1991 by the Policy Economics Group of the economics and consulting firm KPMG Peat Marwick, for the U.S. Council of the Mexico-U.S. Business Committee, analyzed the potential effects of a free trade agreement on 44 distinct business sectors as well as individual households in both the United States and Mexico, utilizing a Computable Generalized Equilibrium model.

55. Ibid.

56. Ibid.

57. Ibid.

58. Ibid.

59. "Telmex is Planning Improvements," *New York Times* (February 26, 1991): D6. Telmex workers are also equity investors, buying a 4.4 percent share in the company with Government financing.

60. "Mexico Puts Three Regional Banks Up for Bids in Privatization Process," *Daily Executive Reporter,* no. 35 (February 21, 1991): A-4.

61. Balassa, *Toward Renewed Economic Growth in Latin America,* 27.

62. "Mexican Government is Offering Tax Breaks for Repatriated Funds," *Wall Street Journal* (June 3, 1989): A8.

63. Mark A. Uhlig, "Mexican Debt Deal May Save Jungle," *New York Times* (February 26, 1991): A3.

64. Sidney Golt, *The GATT Negotiations 1986–90: Origins, Issues, & Prospects* (London: British-North American Committee, 1988), 6.

65. Alejandro Junco, "The Case for an Internal Mexican Free-Trade Agreement," *Wall Street Journal* (March 22, 1991): A9.

66. Asman, "La Perestroika Mexicana," A32.

Bibliography

Adams, W. *The Brain Drain.* New York: Macmillan, 1968.

Adler, E. "Ideological 'Guerrillas' and the Quest for Technological Autonomy: Brazil's Domestic Computer Industry." *International Organization* 40 (Summer 1986): 673–705.

———. "State Institutions, Ideology, and Autonomous Technological Development: Computers and Nuclear Energy in Argentina and Brazil." *Latin American Research Review* 23, no. 2 (1988): 57–90.

Ahluwalia, M. S. "Income Inequality: Some Dimensions of the Problem." In *Redistribution with Growth,* ed. H. Chenery. London: Oxford University Press, 1980, 3–37.

Akeredolu-Ale, E. O. "Environmental, Organizational, and Group Factors in the Evolution of Private Indigenous Entrepreneurship in Nigeria." *Nigerian Journal of Economics and Social Studies* 14 (July 1972): 237–256.

Alisky, M. "Tapping the Resources of Mexico's Underground Economy." *Wall Street Journal* (December 30, 1988): A7.

Alt, J. E., and Chrystal, K. A. *Political Economics.* Los Angeles: University of California Press, 1983.

Asman, D. "La Perestroika Mexicana." *Wall Street Journal* (October 5, 1988): A32.

Balassa, B., et al. *Toward Renewed Economic Growth in Latin America.* Washington, D.C.: Institute for International Economics, 1986.

Bartlett, B. "The World-Wide Tax Revolution." *Wall Street Journal* (August 29, 1989): A16.

Bennett, D., and Sharpe, K. *Transnational Corporations Versus the State: The Political Economy of the Mexican Auto Industry.* Princeton, N.J.: Princeton University Press, 1983.

Berry, A. "Poverty and Inequality in Latin America." *Latin American Research Review* 27, no. 2 (1987): 202–214.

Biersteker, T. J. *Distortion or Development?: Contending Perspectives on the Multinational Corporation.* Cambridge, Mass.: MIT Press, 1978.

Blomstrom, M., and Persson, H. "Foreign Investment and Spillover Efficiency in an Underdeveloped Economy." *World Development* 11, no. 6 (1983): 494–501.

Brannigan, W. "Mexicans Await 'Brady Plan' on Debt, See it Falling Short." *Wall Street Journal* (March 28, 1989): A15.

Britton, J. N. H., and Gilmour, J. M. *The Weakest Link: A Technological Perspective on Canadian Industrial Underdevelopment.* Ottawa: Science Council of Canada, 1978.

Broehl, W. G. "Entrepreneurship in the Less Developed World." See Kent, C. E., 257–271.

Buchele, R. B. *The Development of Small Industrial Entrepreneurs as a Tool of Economic Growth.* Honolulu: Technological and Development Institute, East-West Center, Working Paper Series No. 31, October 1972.

Casson, M. *The Entrepreneur: An Economic Theory.* Totawa, N.J.: Barnes and Noble, 1982.

Cochran, T. C. "Cultural Factors in Economic Growth." *Journal of Economic History* 20 (December 1960): 515–530.

Cohen, R. "Mexican Labor Leader Wields Power to Test President Elect Salinas." *Wall Street Journal* (September 27, 1988): A1.

Cole, A. H. "An Approach to the Study of Entrepreneurship." In *Explorations in Enterprise,* ed. H. G. J. Aitken. Cambridge, Mass.: Harvard University Press, 1985, 30–44.

Committee on the International Migration of Talent. *Modernization and the Migration of Talent.* New York: Education and World Affairs, January 1970.

Dahmien, E. *Entrepreneurial Activity and the Development of Swedish Industry, 1919–1939.* Homewood, Ill.: Irwin, 1970.

Daily Executive Reporter. "Brazilian President Proposes Program to Modernize Industries, Investment." No. 41 (March 1, 1991): A-16.

———. "Mexico Puts Three Regional Banks Up For Bids in Privatization Process." No. 35 (February 21, 1991): A-4.

de Hoogh, J., et al. "Food for a Growing World Population." *European Review of Agricultural Economics* 3 (1977): 455–499.

Diamond, L. "Strategies for Democratization." *Washington Quarterly* 12 (Winter 1989): 141–163.

Dicken, P. *Global Shift: Industrial Change in a Turbulent World.* London: Harper and Row, 1986.

Dixon, W. J. "Progress in Provision of Basic Human Needs: Latin

America, 1960–1980." *Journal of Developing Areas* (January 1987): 129–140.

Doran, C. F. "Structuring the Concept of Dependency Reversal." In *North/South Relations: Studies of Dependency Reversal,* ed. C. F. Doran, et al. New York: Praeger, 1983, 1–27.

Dos Santos, T. "The Structures of Dependency." In *Readings in U.S. Imperialism.* ed. K. T. Fann and D. C. Hodges. Boston: P. Sargent, 1971, 225–237.

Drucker, P. "Multinational Corporations and Developing Countries: Myths and Realities." *Foreign Affairs,* 53 (October 1974): 121–134.

Easterlin, R. "Does Economic Growth Improve the Human Lot?" In *Nations and Households in Economic Growth: Essays in Honor of Moses Abramowitz.* ed. D. Paul and M. Reeder. New York: Academic Press, 1974, 89–125.

Eckbo, P. L. *The Future of World Oil.* Cambridge, Mass.: Ballinger, 1976.

Economic Council of Canada. *The Bottom Line: Technology, Trade, and Income Growth.* Ottawa: Minister of Supply and Services, 1983.

Employment Effects of Multinational Enterprises in Developing Countries. Geneva: International Labour Office, 1981.

Evans, P. B. *Dependent Development: The Alliance of Multinational, State, and Local Capital in Brazil.* Princeton, N.J.: Princeton University Press, 1979.

Fillol, T. R. *Social Factors in Economic Development: The Argentine Case.* Cambridge, Mass.: MIT Press, 1961.

Flemming, W. J. "The Cultural Determinants of Entrepreneurship and Economic Development: A Case Study of Mendoza Province, Argentina, 1861–1914." *Journal of Economic History* 39 (March 1979): 211–224.

Frank, A. G. *Capitalism and Underdevelopment in Latin America: Historical Studies of Chile and Brazil.* New York: Monthly Review Press, 1969.

Franko, L. G., Dixon, M., and Marulanda, C. A. *Entrepreneurship and Industrialization in Latin America.* Studies in Latin American Business, No. 4. Austin: Survey of Business Research, University of Texas, 1966.

Freeman, A. "Private Sector Gets a Boost in Saskatchewan." *Wall Street Journal* (March 28, 1989): A14.

Friedmann, W. G., and Kalmanoff, G. *Joint International Business Ventures*. New York: Columbia University Press, 1961.

Gasse, Y. "Elaborations on the Psychology of the Entrepreneur." See Kent, C. E., 57–65.

Gereffi, G. *The Pharmaceutical Industry and Dependency in the Third World*. Princeton, N.J.: Princeton University Press, 1985.

———. "The Renegotiation of Dependency and the Limits of State Autonomy in Mexico (1975–1980)." See Moran, T. H., 83–106.

Gershenberg, I. "The Training and Spread of Managerial Know-How: A Comparative Analysis of Multinational and Other Firms in Kenya." *World Development* 15 (July 1987): 931–939.

Gilpin, R. *The Political Economy of International Relations*. Princeton, N.J.: Princeton University Press, 1985.

———. *U.S. Power and the Multinational Corporation*. New York: Basic Books, 1975.

Globerman, S. "Canada." Chapter 6 in *Multinational Enterprises, Economic Structures and International Competitiveness*. ed. J. H. Dunning. New York: Wiley, 1958.

Gold, S. *The GATT Negotiations, 1986–1990: Origins, Issues, and Prospects*. London: British-North American Committee, 1988.

Greenfield, S. M., and Strickon, A., eds. *Entrepreneurship and Social Change*. New York: University Press of America, 1986.

Grieco, J. M. "Between Dependency and Autonomy: India's Experience with the International Computer Industry." *International Organization* 36 (Summer 1982): 609–632.

Hagen, E. E. "How Economic Growth Begins: A Theory of Social Change." *Journal of Social Issues* 19 (January 1963): 20–34.

Hampson, F. O. *Forming Economic Policy: The Case of Energy in Canada and Mexico*. New York: St. Martin's, 1986.

Hebert, R. F., and Link, A. N. *The Entrepreneur: Mainstream Views and Radical Critiques*. New York: Praeger, 1982.

Higgins, B. *Economic Development*, revised edition. New York: Norton, 1968.

Hirschman, A. O. *The Strategy of Economic Development*. New Haven, Conn: Yale University Press, 1958.

Hoselitz, B. F. *Sociological Aspects of Economic Growth*. Glencoe, Ill.: The Free Press, 1960.

———. Book review of David McClelland's *The Achieving Society* in *American Journal of Sociology* 68 (July 1962): 132.

Investing in Developing Countries, 5th edition, revised. Paris: Organization for Economic Co-Operation and Development, November 1982.

Junco, A., "The Case for an Internal Mexican Free Trade Agreement." *Wall Street Journal* (March 22, 1991): A9.

Kay, G. *Development and Underdevelopment.* New York: Macmillan, 1975.

Kent, C. E., Sexton, D. L., and Vesper, K. H., eds. *Encyclopedia of Entrepreneurship.* Englewood Cliffs, N.J.: Prentice-Hall, 1982.

Keohane, R. O., and Nye, J. S., Jr. "Power and Interdependency Revisited." *International Organization* 4 (Autumn 1987): 725–753.

Kilby, P. "Hunting the Heffalump." In *Entrepreneurship and Economic Development,* ed. Kilby. New York: The Free Press, 1971, 1–42.

Kirzner, I. M. *Discovery and the Capitalist Process.* Chicago: University of Chicago Press, 1985.

Kobrin, S. J. "Testing the Bargaining Hypothesis in the Manufacturing Sector in Developing Countries." *International Organization* 41 (Autumn 1987): 609–638.

Kravis, B., Heston, A. W., and Summers, R. "The Real G.D.P. Per Capita for More Than 100 Countries." *Economic Journal* 88 (1978): 215–242.

The Largest U.S. Industrial Corporations. Special issue of *Fortune* (April 24, 1989).

Lemco, J. "Economic and Political Development in Modernizing States." *Journal of Developing Societies* 4 (1988): 9–21.

Lewis, W. A. *The Theory of Economic Growth.* London: Allen and Unwin, 1955.

Liebenstein, H. *General X-Efficiency Theory and Economic Development.* New York: Oxford University Press, 1978.

Lipset, S. M. "Values, Education, and Entrepreneurship." In *Elites in Latin America,* ed. Lipset and A. Solari. New York: Oxford University Press, 1963, 3–60.

Little, I. M. D. *Economic Development: Theory, Policy, and International Relations.* New York: Basic Books, 1982.

Maine, H. S., Sir. *Ancient Law: Its Connection with the Early History of Society and its Relations to Modern Ideas.* New York: Holt, 1864. Reprinted, Tucson: University of Arizona Press, 1986.

Marx, K., and Engels, F. *The Communist Manifesto.* Reprinted, London: Pelican, 1967.

Masannat, G. S. "Persistence and Transformation in Traditional Society." *Journal of Developing Societies* 3 (1987): 107–118.

McClelland, D. C. *The Achieving Society*. Princeton, N.J.: Van Nostrand, 1961.

———. "Entrepreneurship and Achievement Motivation." In *Approaches to the Science of Socioeconomic Development,* ed. P. Lengyel. Paris: UNESCO, 1971.

McFetridge, D. G. *Technological Change in Canadian Industry*. Ottawa: Minister of Supply and Services, 1985.

Melnbardis, R., and Malloy, M. T. "Canadian Border Looks Like a Barrier to Takeover Fever." *Wall Street Journal* (September 9, 1989): C12.

"Mexican Government Gives Tax Break for Repatriated Funds." *Wall Street Journal* (August 24, 1989): A7.

"Mexico Woos Foreign Investors and Rejects Them." *Economist* (February 9, 1985): 61–62.

Miller, D. L. "Mexico." See Rushing, F. W., 173–200.

Moffett, M. "Mexico Hopes its Airline Deal Will Be Catalyst." *Wall Street Journal* (August 24, 1989): A7.

Moon, C. "Complex Interdependence and Transnational Lobbying: South Korea in the United States." *International Studies Quarterly* 32 (1988): 67–89.

Moran, T. H., ed. *Multinational Corporations: The Political Economy of Foreign Direct Investment*. Lexington, Mass.: Lexington Books, 1985.

———. "International Political Risk Assessment, Corporate Planning, and Strategies to Offset Political Risk." See Moran, T. H., 107–118.

———. "Multinational Corporations and the Developing Countries: An Analytical Overview." See Moran, T. H., 3–24.

Morawetz, D. *25 Years of Economic Development*. Baltimore: Johns Hopkins University Press, 1977.

Muller, G. P. *Comparative World Data: Statistical Handbook for the Social Sciences*. Baltimore: Johns Hopkins University Press, 1988.

Muller, R. "(More) on Multinational Corporations: Poverty is the Product." *Foreign Policy* 13 (1973–1974): 71–102.

Multinational Enterprises and Social Policy. Geneva: International Labour Office, 1973.

Munoz, H., ed. *From Dependency to Development*. Boulder, Colo.: Westview, 1981.

Murdoch, W. M. *The Poverty of Nations: The Political Economy of Hunger and Population.* Baltimore: Johns Hopkins University Press, 1980.

Newfarmer, R. S. "Multinationals and Marketplace Magic in the 1980s." In *The Political Economy of Development and Underdevelopment.* ed. C. K. Wilber. New York: Random House, 1984, 182–207.

Nordlinger, S. E. "U.S. Cites Three Nations Over Trade." *Baltimore Sun* (May 26, 1989): 1A.

Norris, W. C. *New Frontier for Business Leadership.* Minneapolis, Minn.: Dorn, 1983.

North, D. C. "Beyond the New Economic History." *Journal of Economic History* 34 (March 1974): 1–7.

North, D. C., and Thomas, R. P. *The Rise of the Western World: A New Economic History.* Cambridge: Cambridge University Press, 1973.

Oser, J. *The Evolution of Economic Thought.* New York: Harcourt, Brace and World, 1963.

Philip, G. "The Limitations of Bargaining Theory: A Case Study of the International Petroleum Company in Peru." *World Development* 4 (March 1976): 231–239.

Ramesh, J., and Weiss, C., eds. *Mobilizing Technology for World Development.* New York: Praeger, 1979.

Ricardo, D. *Works and Correspondence,* ed. P. Sraffa. Cambridge: Cambridge University Press, 1952.

Rohter, L. "Mexico Feels Squeeze of Years of Austerity." *New York Times* (July 25, 1989): A1.

Rugman, A. Book review of Thomas Biersteker's *Distortion or Development?* in *Political Science Quarterly* 94 (Winter 1980): 723–724.

Rushing, F. W., and Brown, C. G., eds *National Policies for Developing High Technology Industries.* Boulder, Colo.: Westview, 1986.

Sauvant, K. P. *Trade and Foreign Direct Investment in Data Services.* Boulder, Colo: Westview, 1986.

Say, J. *Catechism of Political Economy.* London, 1816.

———. *A Treatise on Political Economy.* London, 1821.

Schafer, M. "Capturing the Mineral Multinationals: Advantage or Disadvantage?" See Moran, T. H., 25–54.

Schatz, S. P., "*n* Achievement and Economic Growth: A Critical Appraisal." In *Entrepreneurship and Economic Development,* ed. P. Kilby. New York: The Free Press, 1971, 183–190.

Schumpeter, J. A. *The Theory of Economic Development*. Cambridge, Mass.: Harvard University Press, 1934.

Schwartzman, S. "The Power of Technology." *Latin American Research Review* 24, no. 1 (1989): 209–221.

Scott, R. "Political Elites." See Lipset, S. M., 117–145.

Sethi, S., and Sheth, J., eds. *Multinational Business Operations I*. Pacific Palisades, Calif.: Goodyear Publishing Co., 1973.

Siegel, B. J. "Social Structures and Economic Change in Brazil." In *Economic Growth: Brazil, India, Japan*, ed. S. S. Kuznets. Durham, N.C.: Duke University Press, 1955, 388–411.

Singh, D. B., *Economics of Development*. New York: Asia Publishing House, 1966.

Smith, A. *An Inquiry into the Nature and Causes of the Wealth of Nations*, 2 volumes. London: Printed for W. Strahan and T. Cadell, 1776. Republished, E. Cannan, ed., 1 volume, New York: Random House, Modern Library Edition, 1937.

Smith, S. "Entrepreneurial Agriculture and the Involution of Agricultural Dynamics in the Americas." In *Entrepreneurship and Social Change: Monographs in Economic Anthropology No. 2*, ed. S. M. Greenfield and A. Strickon. Lanham, Md.: University Press of America, 1986, 96–123.

Stepan, A. C. *The State and Society: Peru in Comparative Perspective*. Princeton, N.J.: Princeton University Press, 1978.

Story, D. *Industry, the State, and Public Policy in Mexico*. Austin: University of Texas Press, 1986.

Straasman, W. P. "The Industrialist." In *Continuity and Change in Latin America*. ed. J. J. Johnson. Stanford: Stanford University Press, 1964, 161–185.

Sunkel, O. "Big Business and Dependencia." *Foreign Affairs* 52 (April 1972): 517–531.

Sutcliffe, R. *Industry and Development*. London: Addison Wesley, 1983.

Tarasofsky, A. *The Subsidization of Innovative Projects by the Government of Canada*. Ottawa: Supply and Services Canada, 1984.

"Taxing Time." *Economist*, Canadian survey issue (October 8, 1988): 11–12.

"Telmex is Planning Improvements." *New York Times* (February 26, 1991): D6.

Thurow, R. "Africa's Poorest Nations Press Debt Relief." *Wall Street Journal* (September 21, 1988): A22.

Tripathi, D. "Occupational Mobility and Indigenous Entrepreneurship in India: A Historical Analysis." *Developing Economies* 19 (March 1981): 52–68.

Tuma, E. H. "Institutionalized Obstacles to Development: The Case of Egypt." *World Development* 16, no. 10 (1988): 1185–1198.

Uhlig, M.A., "Mexican Debt Deal May Save Jungle." *New York Times* (February 26, 1991): A3.

Valenzuela, J. S., and Valenzuela, A. V. "Modernization and Dependency: Alternative Perspectives in the Study of Latin American Development." See Munoz, H., 15–42.

Vernon, R. "The Economic Consequences of U.S. Foreign Direct Investment." In Vernon, *Economic and Political Consequences of the Multinational Enterprise: An Anthology*. Boston: Division of Research, Harvard Business School, 1972, 75.

———. *Multinational Enterprises in Developing Countries: An Analysis of National Goals and Policies*. Working paper. Boston: Harvard Institute of International Development, June 1975.

———. *The Operations of Multinational U.S. Enterprises in Developing Countries*. New York: United Nations UNCTAD TD/B/ 399, 1972.

Wanniski, J. *The Way The World Works: How Economies Fail—and Succeed*. New York: Basic Books, 1978.

Wareham, M. *Looking Back, Reaching Forward: A History of Computing Devices Company*. Ottawa: Undated in-house publication of Computing Devices, Division of Control Data Corporation, Canada.

Warren, B. *Imperialism: Pioneer of Capitalism*. London: NLB, 1980.

Weaver, J. H., and Berger, M. "The Marxist Critique of Dependency Theory." In *The Political Economy of Development and Underdevelopment*, 3d edition, ed. C. K. Wilber. New York: Random House, 1984, 45–63.

Weber, M. *The Protestant Ethic and the Spirit of Capitalism*, trans. T. Parsons. London: Allen and Unwin, 1970.

Westphal, L. E., Yung, W. P., and Parsell, G. "Foreign Influences on Korean Industrial Development." *Oxford Bulletin of Economics and Statistics* 41 (November 1979): 359–388.

Wilber, C. K. "Methodological Debate in Economics: Editor's Introduction." *World Development* 14 (February 1986): 143–145.

Wisman, J. D. "The Methodology of W. Arthur Lewis's Development Economics." *World Development* 14 (February 1986): 165–180.

World Bank. *World Development Report 1982*. New York: Oxford
    University Press, 1982.
The World in Figures. London: Economist Publications, 1985.

Index